I0412759

U.S. Department of
Transportation
**Federal Railroad
Administration**

Assessment of Risks for High-Speed Rail Grade Crossings on the Empire Corridor

Office of Research and
Development
Washington, DC 20590

Next Generation High-Speed Rail Program

Research and Special Programs Administration
John A. Volpe National Transportation Systems Center
Cambridge, MA 02142-1093

DOT/FRA/RDV-00/05
DOT-VNTSC-FRA-00-03

Final Report
August 2000

This document is available to the public through the National Technical Information Service, Springfield, VA 22161. This document is also available on the FRA web site at www.fra.dot.gov.

REPORT DOCUMENTATION PAGE

Form Approved
OMB No. 0704-0188

Public reporting burden for this collection of information is estimated to average 1 hour per response, including the time for reviewing instructions, searching existing data sources, gathering and maintaining the data needed, and completing and reviewing the collection of information. Send comments regarding this burden estimate or any other aspect of this collection of information, including suggestions for reducing this burden, to Washington Headquarters Services, Directorate for Information Operations and Reports, 1215 Jefferson Davis Highway, Suite 1204, Arlington, VA 22202-4302, and to the Office of Management and Budget, Paperwork Reduction Project (0704-0188), Washington, DC 20503.

1. AGENCY USE ONLY (Leave blank)	2. REPORT DATE August 2000	3. REPORT TYPE AND DATES COVERED Final Report

4. TITLE AND SUBTITLE Assessment of Risks for High-Speed Rail Grade Crossings on the Empire Corridor	5. FUNDING NUMBERS RR003/R0047
6. AUTHOR(S) Mark Mironer, Michael Coltman, and Robert McCown (FRA)	

7. PERFORMING ORGANIZATION NAME(S) AND ADDRESS(ES) U.S. Department of Transportation Research and Special Programs Administration John A. Volpe National Transportation Systems Center Cambridge, MA 02142-1093	8. PERFORMING ORGANIZATION REPORT NUMBER DOT-VNTSC-FRA-00-03

9. SPONSORING/MONITORING AGENCY NAME(S) AND ADDRESS(ES) U.S. Department of Transportation Federal Railroad Administration Office of Railroad Development 1120 Vermont Avenue, NW Mail Stop 20 Washington, D.C. 20590	10. SPONSORING/MONITORING AGENCY REPORT NUMBER DOT/FRA/RDV-00/05

11. SUPPLEMENTARY NOTES

12a. DISTRIBUTION/AVAILABILITY STATEMENT This document is available to the public through the National Technical Information Service, Springfield, VA 22161. This document is also available on the FRA web site at www.fra.dot.gov.	12b. DISTRIBUTION CODE

13. ABSTRACT (Maximum 200 words)

The report describes a risk-based approach for assessing the implications of higher train speeds on highway-railroad grade crossing safety, and allocating limited resources to best reduce this risk. To predict accident frequency, an existing DOT model was extended to include higher speeds. Accidents were statistically grouped according to crash mechanics. By using historical data and crashworthiness analysis, the severity of an accident was estimated independently for the highway users and train occupants based on a number of factors. These included accident type, type of highway vehicle, type of train, and train speed.

The Empire Corridor in New York State was used to illustrate the application of the approach. The study concludes that the increased risk due to higher train speeds can often be more than offset by implementing standard crossing improvements. The analysis shows that improving the highest risk crossings in a corridor, rather than the crossings with the highest train speed, produces the greatest benefit. The report finds that the risk to highway users saturates at train speeds around 65 mph, and that the risk to train occupants does not increase dramatically with train speed. The report recommends an incremental migration to improved safety.

14. SUBJECT TERMS High-speed rail, grade crossing, highway-rail intersection, risk assessment, corridor assessment, Empire Corridor, Amtrak, New York State, Federal Railroad Administration, FRA.	15. NUMBER OF PAGES 50
	16. PRICE CODE

17. SECURITY CLASSIFICATION OF REPORT Unclassified	18. SECURITY CLASSIFICATION OF THIS PAGE Unclassified	19. SECURITY CLASSIFICATION OF ABSTRACT Unclassified	20. LIMITATION OF ABSTRACT

NSN 7540-01-280-5500

Standard Form 298 (Rev. 2-89)
Prescribed by ANSI Std. 239-18
298-102

REPORT DOCUMENTATION PAGE

Form Approved
OMB No. 0704-0188

Public reporting burden for this collection of information is estimated to average 1 hour per response, including the time for reviewing instructions, searching existing data sources, gathering and maintaining the data needed, and completing and reviewing the collection of information. Send comments regarding this burden estimate or any other aspect of this collection of information, including suggestions for reducing this burden, to Washington Headquarters Services, Directorate for Information Operations and Reports, 1215 Jefferson Davis Highway, Suite 1204, Arlington, VA 22202-4302, and to the Office of Management and Budget, Paperwork Reduction Project (0704-0188), Washington, DC 20503.

1. AGENCY USE ONLY (Leave blank)	2. REPORT DATE August 2000	3. REPORT TYPE AND DATES COVERED Final Report

4. TITLE AND SUBTITLE Assessment of Risks for High-Speed Rail Grade Crossings on the Empire Corridor	5. FUNDING NUMBERS RR003/R0047
6. AUTHOR(S) Mark Mironer, Michael Coltman, and Robert McCown (FRA)	

7. PERFORMING ORGANIZATION NAME(S) AND ADDRESS(ES) U.S. Department of Transportation Research and Special Programs Administration John A. Volpe National Transportation Systems Center Cambridge, MA 02142-1093	8. PERFORMING ORGANIZATION REPORT NUMBER DOT-VNTSC-FRA-00-03

9. SPONSORING/MONITORING AGENCY NAME(S) AND ADDRESS(ES) U.S. Department of Transportation Federal Railroad Administration Office of Railroad Development 1120 Vermont Avenue, NW Mail Stop 20 Washington, D.C. 20590	10. SPONSORING/MONITORING AGENCY REPORT NUMBER DOT/FRA/RDV-00/05

11. SUPPLEMENTARY NOTES

12a. DISTRIBUTION/AVAILABILITY STATEMENT This document is available to the public through the National Technical Information Service, Springfield, VA 22161. This document is also available on the FRA web site at www.fra.dot.gov.	12b. DISTRIBUTION CODE

13. ABSTRACT (Maximum 200 words)

The report describes a risk-based approach for assessing the implications of higher train speeds on highway-railroad grade crossing safety, and allocating limited resources to best reduce this risk. To predict accident frequency, an existing DOT model was extended to include higher speeds. Accidents were statistically grouped according to crash mechanics. By using historical data and crashworthiness analysis, the severity of an accident was estimated independently for the highway users and train occupants based on a number of factors. These included accident type, type of highway vehicle, type of train, and train speed.

The Empire Corridor in New York State was used to illustrate the application of the approach. The study concludes that the increased risk due to higher train speeds can often be more than offset by implementing standard crossing improvements. The analysis shows that improving the highest risk crossings in a corridor, rather than the crossings with the highest train speed, produces the greatest benefit. The report finds that the risk to highway users saturates at train speeds around 65 mph, and that the risk to train occupants does not increase dramatically with train speed. The report recommends an incremental migration to improved safety.

14. SUBJECT TERMS High-speed rail, grade crossing, highway-rail intersection, risk assessment, corridor assessment, Empire Corridor, Amtrak, New York State, Federal Railroad Administration, FRA.	15. NUMBER OF PAGES 50
	16. PRICE CODE

17. SECURITY CLASSIFICATION OF REPORT Unclassified	18. SECURITY CLASSIFICATION OF THIS PAGE Unclassified	19. SECURITY CLASSIFICATION OF ABSTRACT Unclassified	20. LIMITATION OF ABSTRACT

NSN 7540-01-280-5500

Standard Form 298 (Rev. 2-89)
Prescribed by ANSI Std. 239-18
298-102

PREFACE

Highway-rail intersections or at-grade crossings are numerous in emerging high-speed corridors, averaging more than one crossing per mile of track. While the existing U.S. methodology for determining appropriate grade crossing warning devices is risk based, it does not fully address high-speed operations. Recent guidelines have been published recommending grade separation or fail-safe, full-barrier systems with vehicle detection technology. The cost of grade separation, or the full-barrier systems, may be a significant impediment to the introduction of high-speed service. If the objective is to reduce risk while improving rail passenger service, careful corridor-based analyses are required to achieve the greatest benefit within the limited budgets available for most of these projects.

This report is intended to give the reader a better understanding of the sources of risk in a high-speed corridor and show how these sources of risk change with increased train speeds. The report then evaluates the effectiveness of competing risk reduction alternatives.

This report was prepared by the Volpe National Transportation Systems Center in support of the United States Department of Transportation, Federal Railroad Administration's (FRA) Office of Railroad Development. The authors wish to thank Grady Cothen and Bruce George of the FRA's Office of Safety, and Richard McDonough of the New York State Department of Transportation for their assistance and critical review during the conduct of this study.

METRIC/ENGLISH CONVERSION FACTORS

ENGLISH TO METRIC

LENGTH (APPROXIMATE)

1 inch (in) = 2.5 centimeters (cm)

1 foot (ft) = 30 centimeters (cm)

1 yard (yd) = 0.9 meter (m)

1 mile (mi) = 1.6 kilometers (km)

AREA (APPROXIMATE)

1 square inch (sq in, in^2) = 6.5 square centimeters (cm^2)

1 square foot (sq ft, ft^2) = 0.09 square meter (m^2)

1 square yard (sq yd, yd^2) = 0.8 square meter (m^2)

1 square mile (sq mi, mi^2) = 2.6 square kilometers (km^2)

1 acre = 0.4 hectare (he) = 4,000 square meters (m^2)

MASS - WEIGHT (APPROXIMATE)

1 ounce (oz) = 28 grams (gm)

1 pound (lb) = 0.45 kilogram (kg)

1 short ton = 2,000 pounds (lb) = 0.9 tonne (t)

VOLUME (APPROXIMATE)

1 teaspoon (tsp) = 5 milliliters (ml)

1 tablespoon (tbsp) = 15 milliliters (ml)

1 fluid ounce (fl oz) = 30 milliliters (ml)

1 cup (c) = 0.24 liter (l)

1 pint (pt) = 0.47 liter (l)

1 quart (qt) = 0.96 liter (l)

1 gallon (gal) = 3.8 liters (l)

1 cubic foot (cu ft, ft^3) = 0.03 cubic meter (m^3)

1 cubic yard (cu yd, yd^3) = 0.76 cubic meter (m^3)

TEMPERATURE (EXACT)

$[(x-32)(5/9)]$ °F = y °C

METRIC TO ENGLISH

LENGTH (APPROXIMATE)

1 millimeter (mm) = 0.04 inch (in)

1 centimeter (cm) = 0.4 inch (in)

1 meter (m) = 3.3 feet (ft)

1 meter (m) = 1.1 yards (yd)

1 kilometer (km) = 0.6 mile (mi)

AREA (APPROXIMATE)

1 square centimeter (cm^2) = 0.16 square inch (sq in, in^2)

1 square meter (m^2) = 1.2 square yards (sq yd, yd^2)

1 square kilometer (km^2) = 0.4 square mile (sq mi, mi^2)

10,000 square meters (m^2) = 1 hectare (ha) = 2.5 acres

MASS - WEIGHT (APPROXIMATE)

1 gram (gm) = 0.036 ounce (oz)

1 kilogram (kg) = 2.2 pounds (lb)

1 tonne (t) = 1,000 kilograms (kg)

= 1.1 short tons

VOLUME (APPROXIMATE)

1 milliliter (ml) = 0.03 fluid ounce (fl oz)

1 liter (l) = 2.1 pints (pt)

1 liter (l) = 1.06 quarts (qt)

1 liter (l) = 0.26 gallon (gal)

1 cubic meter (m^3) = 36 cubic feet (cu ft, ft^3)

1 cubic meter (m^3) = 1.3 cubic yards (cu yd, yd^3)

TEMPERATURE (EXACT)

$[(9/5) y + 32]$ °C = x °F

QUICK INCH - CENTIMETER LENGTH CONVERSION

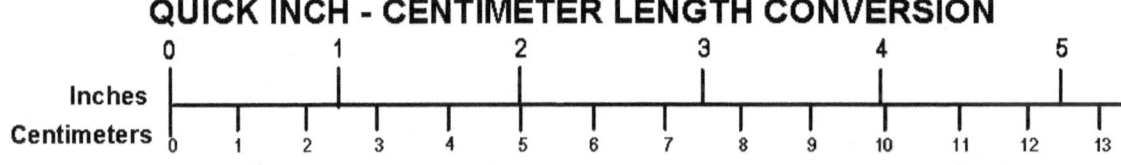

QUICK FAHRENHEIT - CELSIUS TEMPERATURE CONVERSION

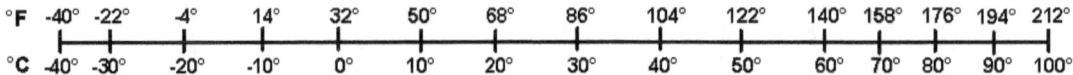

For more exact and or other conversion factors, see NIST Miscellaneous Publication 286, Units of Weights and Measures. Price $2.50 SD Catalog No. C13 10286

Updated 6/17/98

iv

TABLE OF CONTENTS

TABLE OF CONTENTS (Cont.)

LIST OF FIGURES

LIST OF FIGURES (Cont.)

LIST OF TABLES

1. INTRODUCTION

1.1 PURPOSE

This study develops a risk-based approach for assessing the implications of higher train speeds on highway-railroad grade crossing safety and allocating limited resources to best reduce this risk. While it is reasonable to assume that increasing train speed at any individual crossing will increase the risk to both train and highway vehicle occupants, the magnitude of this increase, especially relative to the risk at other crossings, is less clear. With limited resources to apply to grade crossing improvements, it is important that the available funds be spent where they will do the most good. This analysis shows where opportunities for greatest improvements are located.

A section of the Empire Corridor in New York State is used to illustrate the application of this approach.

1.2 BACKGROUND

High-speed rail passenger service is being encouraged in the United States as evidenced by legislation such as the Intermodal Surface Transportation Efficiency Act of 1991 (ISTEA), the Swift Rail Development Act of 1994, the Transportation Equity Act for the 21st Century (TEA 21), and the FRA's Next Generation High-Speed Rail Program. As a result of this legislation and other initiatives, 10 high-speed rail passenger service corridors have been designated in the United States. High-speed rail operations on these and other emerging corridors could eventually result in train speeds above 110 mph. These higher train speeds, resulting in shorter trip times, are important in attracting new riders to passenger rail. While higher speeds and greater numbers of trains without improvements in warning devices at crossings will increase the risk to both highway vehicle occupants and train passengers and crew, there are also many public benefits to higher speeds, including diversion of highway travelers from congested roads onto trains. The goal is to attain this improvement in service while reducing the risk to both rail and highway users.

Historically, crossing improvements have been implemented incrementally. Efforts have included the standardization and implementation of crossbucks, lights, and gates. As high-risk crossings were identified, first through an examination of accident data, then through the use of risk assessment techniques, the warning devices were upgraded at high-risk crossings, or the crossings were closed, or were grade separated. Once the risk was reduced at these highest-risk crossings, the next highest-risk crossings were addressed, and so on. In some cases, use of more effective warning devices has improved safety, making increases in train speed acceptable, with the improved service leading to greater revenues and ultimately more funds being available for more safety improvements.

Only recently has train speed been a focus in terms of risk. The FRA sponsored a study conducted by Battelle [1] under the direction of the Volpe Center to review international methodologies for evaluating and improving the effectiveness of grade crossings, warning devices, and crossing barriers. The study showed that many countries use risk assessment techniques to assess individual crossings, but rarely quantify corridor impacts or other optimization strategies.

The FRA does not specifically require the installation of special warning devices at grade crossings. Standard highway practices require at least crossbucks on public crossings. Recognizing that these risks must be addressed if high- speed rail service is to be realized, the FRA has proposed guidelines for the installation of motorist warning and train protection devices at grade crossings on the designated high-speed rail corridors. In summary, the FRA Guidelines call for the actions shown in Table 1-1.

Table 1-1. FRA Guidelines

Rail Speed (mph)	Public Crossings	Private Crossings
80 to 110	Eliminate all redundant or unnecessary crossings. Install the most sophisticated traffic control/warning devices compatible with the location, e.g., median barriers, special signing, four-quadrant gates. Automated devices should be equipped with constant warning time equipment.	Close, grade separate, or provide a secured barrier or automatic devices for private crossings. Device or barrier should extend across the entire highway on both sides of the track, should normally be closed and opened on request, if no train is approaching, for a period of time sufficient to cross the tracks.
111 to 125	Protect rail movement with full width barriers capable of absorbing impact of highway vehicle. Include a fail-safe vehicle detection capability between barriers. Notify approaching trains of warning device or barrier failure, or of an intruding vehicle in sufficient time for the train to stop short of the crossing without resorting to emergency brake application.	Protect rail movement with full width barrier or gate, normally closed and locked, capable of absorbing impact of a highway vehicle. Gate lock or control should be interlocked with train signal and control system and released by a railroad dispatcher. A fail-safe vehicle detection or video system should monitor the area between the barriers. The crossing should be equipped with a direct link telephone to the railroad dispatcher.
Above 125	Close or grade separate all highway-rail crossings.	Close or grade separate all highway-rail crossings.

The implementation of these guidelines would result in a significant level of risk reduction. In the case of grade separation for speeds exceeding 125 mph, the risks will be reduced to essentially zero. The 111 to 125 mph section for public crossings is more ambiguous. There are currently no widely available devices that satisfy these requirements which may necessitate grade separation to satisfy the guidelines. There are significant cost impacts associated with implementation of the guidelines on the designated high-speed rail corridors. These corridors include about 2,000 public and 900 private crossings over some 3,000 route miles. At a cost of $3 million for a typical grade separation, upgrading these crossings to the requirements of the guidelines will incur significant costs and exhibit other impacts to the states, communities, and railroads affected. The high cost of these safety requirements could serve as a significant impediment to furthering the implementation of high-speed rail service. Other motorist warning and train protection device alternatives applied in a "corridor" approach may achieve similar levels of risk at a much lower cost.

It should also be noted that while the guidelines present recommendations for speeds under 110 mph, the practice has been to apply less costly warnings, if any, at such crossings. A large effort would be required to bring all crossings into compliance with these guidelines, even at present train speeds.

While the guidelines are an excellent ultimate goal, given limited budgets for grade crossing improvements, an incremental approach is needed to reach that goal. By focusing on the highest-risk crossings regardless of train speed, safety can be incrementally improved as much as resources allow until the goals are reached.

In 1998, the FRA finalized new track safety standards (June 22, 1998). In these new rules, the FRA requires a carrier to submit warning or protection plans for crossings where the speeds are authorized above 110 mph. The High-Speed Track Safety Standards, Federal Register, CFR 49, Part 213.347 (b)[2] state:

> If train operation is projected at Class 7 speed for a track segment that will include rail-highway grade crossings, the track owner shall submit for FRA's approval a complete description of the proposed warning/barrier system to address the protection of highway traffic and high-speed trains.

An important aspect of the required submittal might include an estimate of corridor risk. The new high-speed standards prohibit crossings where track speeds exceed 125 mph.

1.3   RISK

The concept of 'risk' requires some explanation. Risk is the product of the probability of an event occurring, and the severity of that event. The units of these terms vary greatly from study to study. In this report, the probability is defined as the predicted number of grade crossing accidents along a certain set of crossings per year. The severity is defined in terms of fatalities (both on the train and highway vehicle) per accident. Therefore, the risk in this study is defined as predicted fatalities per year at that set of crossings.

Other possible measures of severity include injuries, property damage, and other impacts and costs, such as delays and public perception. Fatalities were chosen as being an essential measure of safety without some of the ambiguity involved in injury counts. The other measures are open to even more interpretation, although it is likely that the crossings where the most fatalities occur also would be the most risky by these other measures as well.

Since risk is the product of these two quantities, if at one crossing there is one accident per year with one fatality, and at another crossing there is only one accident every 10 years, but there are ten fatalities in that crash, the statistical risk is the same at each crossing – one fatality per year.

1.4 OUTLINE

Sections 2 through 4 describe the methods used in this analysis. Section 2 focuses on the accident prediction model and Section 3 on the severity model. Section 4 presents the costs and effectiveness of crossing warning alternatives. Section 5 applies these models to a set of crossings in New York, the Empire Corridor. Finally, Section 6 summarizes these results, and presents recommendations.

2. ACCIDENT PREDICTION MODEL

2.1 INTRODUCTION

The first half of the risk equation is accident probability or frequency. The chance of an accident at a particular crossing varies depending on many of the characteristics of the crossing itself. To predict accident frequency, an existing DOT model was used [3]. Since the model is described and validated in depth in the referenced report, this section will present only a brief overview of the model.

It should also be noted that since the overall analysis approach is modular, it is quite easy to substitute another accident prediction model, such as one specific to the site being examined.

2.2 OVERVIEW OF MODEL

The model was derived by "applying nonlinear multiple regression techniques to crossing characteristics stored in the US DOT/FRA Highway-Rail Grade Crossing Inventory and to accident data contained in the FRA Railroad Accident/Incident Reporting System." [4] This approach yielded a formula that would predict the probable number of accidents at a given crossing, based on the data found in the Inventory. The equation is dominated by the exposure index term that combines the average daily traffic count and the number of trains. This equation is:

$$a = K \times EI \times MT \times DT \times HP \times MS \times HL$$

where,

a = un-normalized accident prediction (accidents/year at the crossing)
K = constant for initialization of factor values at 1.00
EI = factor for exposure index based on product of highway and train traffic
MT = factor for number of main tracks
DT = factor for number of through trains per day during daylight
HP = highway paved factor
MS = factor for maximum timetable speed
HL = factor for number of highway lanes

Table 2-1 gives the formulas to determine each of these factors based on the data in the Inventory.

Table 2-1. Crossing Characteristic Factors

Crossing Category	Formula Constant K	Exposure Index EI	Main Tracks Factor MT	Day Thru Trains Factor DT	Highway Paved Factor HP	Max Speed Factor MS	Highway Lanes Factor HL
Passive	0.0006938	$\left(\dfrac{c \cdot t + 0.2}{0.2}\right)^{0.37}$	1	$\left(\dfrac{d + 0.2}{0.2}\right)^{0.178}$	$e^{-0.5966(hp-1)}$	$e^{0.0077ms}$	1.0
Flashing Lights	0.0003351	$\left(\dfrac{c \cdot t + 0.2}{0.2}\right)^{0.4106}$	$e^{0.1917mt}$	$\left(\dfrac{d + 0.2}{0.2}\right)^{0.1131}$	1.0	1.0	$e^{0.1826(hl-1)}$
Gates	0.0005745	$\left(\dfrac{c \cdot t + 0.2}{0.2}\right)^{0.2942}$	$e^{0.1512mt}$	$\left(\dfrac{d + 0.2}{0.2}\right)^{0.1781}$	1.0	1.0	$e^{0.1420(hl-1)}$

General Form of Accident Prediction Formula: $a = K \times EI \times MT \times DT \times HP \times MS \times HL$

c = annual average number of highway vehicles per day (total both directions)
t = average total train movements per day
mt = number of main tracks
d = average number of through trains per day during daylight
hp = highway paved (yes = 1, no = 2)
ms = maximum timetable speed, mph
ht = highway type factor value
hl = number of highway lanes

To obtain the normalized value, one must multiply the predicted value by the appropriate normalizing constant found in each year's Highway-Rail Crossing Accident/Incident and Inventory Bulletin. These constants were last modified in 1992, and were 0.8239 for passive crossings, 0.6935 for crossings with flashing lights, and 0.6714 for gated crossings.

There are several notes regarding this model. First, the referenced report describes how the accident prediction, as found from the above equation, should be weighted with the actual accident history to obtain a more accurate prediction estimate. In determining the effect of increasing speeds at a given crossing, however, the history is no longer applicable, and so the un-weighted prediction is used here. Additionally, while the preferred method of obtaining an estimate for the accident rate, when the protection on a crossing is improved, is to apply an effectiveness rate to the baseline prediction, once again, because of the changed speeds, this method was not used. Instead, the accident rate is predicted from the foregoing equations.

6

As mentioned previously, the model was derived by applying regression techniques to the data in the grade crossing inventory. There may be crossing characteristics that affect accident probability that are not included in the inventory, such as sight distance and crossing geometry – they do not appear in the model. The model does not distinguish between freight and passenger trains, since the distinction is not made in the inventory. While the model does incorporate many factors, it should be noted that the dominant variables are the type of crossing warning, and the train and highway vehicle traffic density.

The regression showed that for Flashing Lights and Gates, train speed does not affect accident probability. The implication for this analysis is that at higher speeds, the increase in risk is due entirely to severity, rather than accident probability.

Since the model was based on historical accident data, it could not have been verified on the higher speeds being considered here. To assume that the insensitivity to train speed at active crossings that holds from 0 to 80 mph extends to higher speeds as well seems reasonable, however. Similarly, using the same formula for passive crossings at speeds above 80 mph, as is used at lower speeds, is the best approximation at the present time.

Finally, although the accident prediction model includes a severity calculation, it was not used here for several reasons. First, there is no differentiation between freight trains and passenger trains (the latter have a much greater severity potential). Secondly, the output is the likelihood of a fatal accident, not a prediction of numbers of fatalities, which is needed for this risk analysis. Third, the model was not designed for higher speed accidents, and since the focus of this study is the risk at such crossings, an independent severity model was needed.

Accident probability, the first element of risk, is calculated as described above. The next step is to determine the severity as a function of train speed, which will be described in the following section.

3. SEVERITY MODELING

3.1   INTRODUCTION

In generating a model of severity as a function of train speed, the authors attempted to be as realistic as possible, while still being confident that the actual severity could be no worse than that which is predicted. There have been too few grade crossing accidents involving high-speed trains to provide significant statistics directly indicating severity. Therefore, wherever possible, the FRA data bases of accidents at lower speeds were used as a starting point.

The severity model is modular, so that if new data become available, the model can be easily changed to incorporate the refinements.

3.2   APPROACH

The severity of a grade crossing accident depends on a number of factors, including accident type, type of highway vehicle, type of train, and train speed. In order to model severity, accidents were statistically broken down into categories with distinct crash mechanics. Each of these categories could then be examined using historical data, statistics, and crashworthiness analysis to predict severity. This approach is illustrated on Figure 3-1.

The first part of Figure 3-1 is the top level tree, where accidents are broken into the two main branches; Train Striking Highway Vehicle and Highway Vehicle Striking Train.

Since this analysis focuses on high-speed rail operations and is intended to set an upper bound for risk, it was assumed that all trains involved in the predicted accidents were passenger trains, and that the trains traveled at the maximum allowable track speed.

The middle section of Figure 3-1 shows the breakdown of the highway-vehicle-into-train crash mode. Since autos, trucks and truck-trailers account for 99.1 percent of the grade crossing accidents involving passenger trains (excluding pedestrians and unspecified vehicles), only those three categories are considered in this analysis. As can be seen from the figure, in each case, some harm to both the train and the highway vehicle is generated from the impact itself. Then, if the accident causes a derailment, additional harm may be realized.

The final section of Figure 3-1, the tree structure for train-into-highway-vehicle, is based on a similar logic.

The following section describes how the values of harm for each branch of the tree were determined.

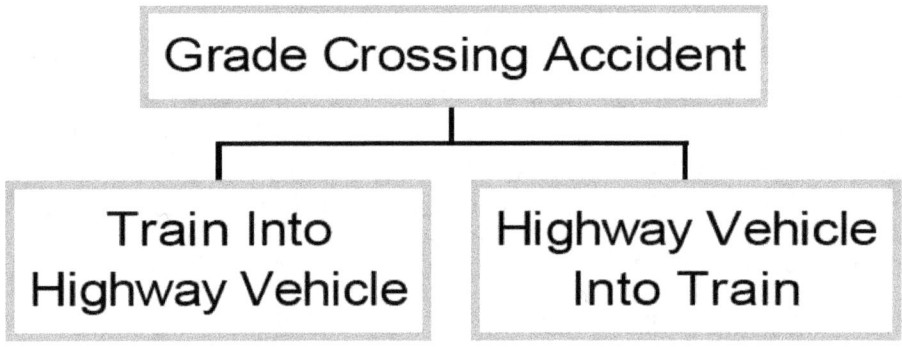

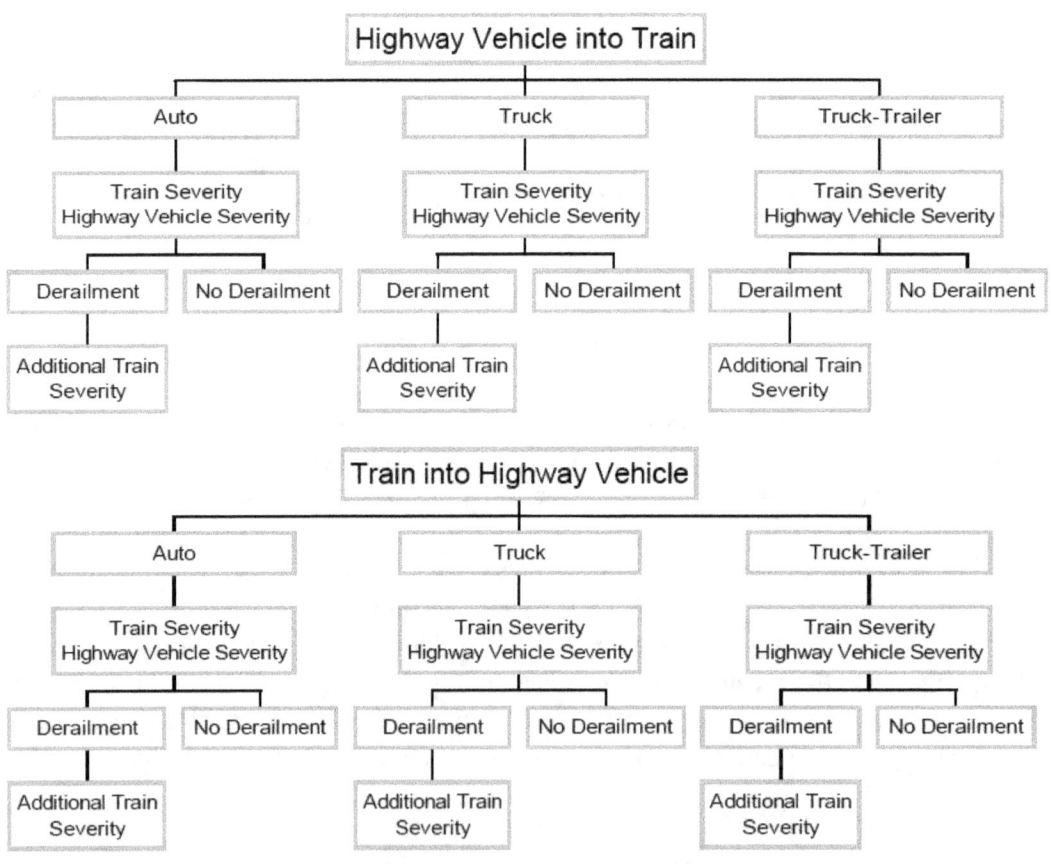

Figure 3-1. Severity Element Breakdown

3.3   SEVERITY OF CRASH SCENARIOS

The severity models were based on the crash data bases and were supplemented with engineering analysis where necessary.

3.3.1   Train Into Highway Vehicle

The harm to the highway vehicle is considered first. As expected, the accident data show that the severity generally increases with increasing train speed. Between 70 and 80 mph, the severity levels off, presumably because the maximum harm for the impact location is being done to the highway vehicle and increased speed cannot do more damage. The number is somewhat less than the average occupancy since some accidents are survivable regardless of train speed. For example, if the train just "nicks" the front of the highway vehicle, then most often there will be no fatalities even at high train speeds. Since the severity of the impact is related to the kinetic energy involved, a quadratic relationship was used to model the severity below the peak speed. Figures 3-2, 3-3, and 3-4 show the modeled curve compared to the actual data for the three vehicle types. Since the train speeds of greatest interest to this analysis are between 80 and 125 mph, the quadratic relationships do not affect those results but are included for completeness.

The accident data base was first analyzed to model fatalities on the train. Of the 9,615 passenger train grade crossing accidents between 1975 and 1995, there were 42 deaths of train occupants (including crew). This represents an historical severity rate of about 0.00437 fatalities per accident. However, 34 of these fatalities occurred between 1975 and 1978. Most likely this dramatic change in fatality rate is due to the improvements in train crashworthiness and crossing warnings that were applied in this time period. From 1979 through 1995, there were 8 fatalities in the 6,742 accidents, for a rate of 0.0019 fatalities per accident. With such a small number of fatalities, it was not possible to derive a relationship between train speed and fatalities on the train. Instead, it was again assumed that harm to the train was related to kinetic energy and hence quadratic in form [5]. Furthermore, the crash energy is related to the mass of the vehicle struck, so one would expect the severity when striking an auto to be less than striking a truck, which in turn is less than striking a truck-trailer. Figure 3-5 shows the relationship representing the severity of striking each type of vehicle.

For purposes of this study, a conservative severity relationship was assumed. For example, Figure 3-5 shows that the severity to train occupants of a truck-trailer collision at 80 mph is about 0.28 fatalities per accident. In the data base, there were 104 accidents involving truck-trailers at train speeds of 71-80 mph from 1975-95, resulting in 6 fatalities of train occupants, a rate of 0.06 fatalities per accident. But the potentially higher probability of a catastrophic crash involving this type of vehicle justifies this conservative estimate.

11

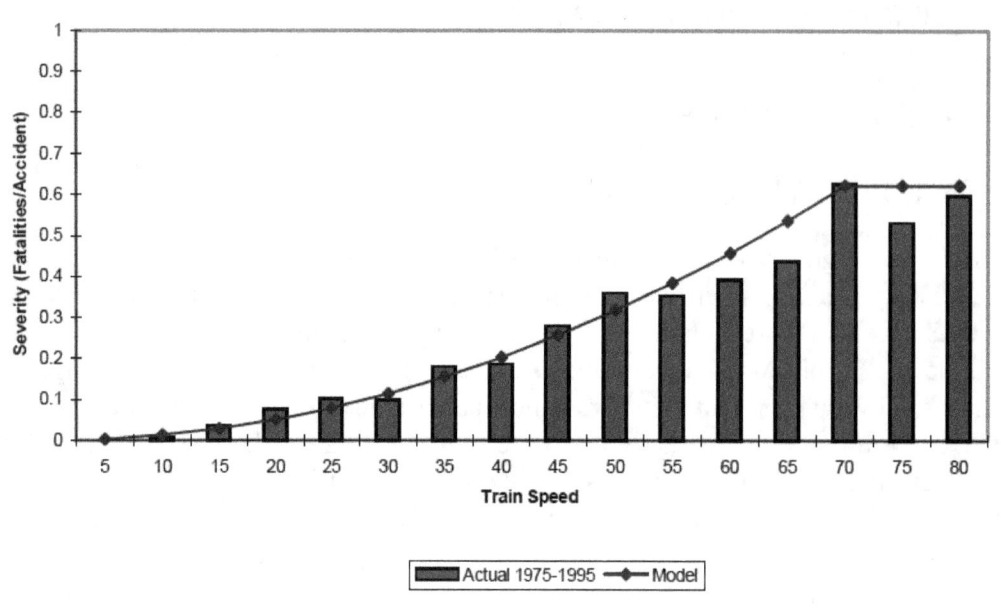

Figure 3-2. Fatalities per Accident on Autos Struck by Passenger Train

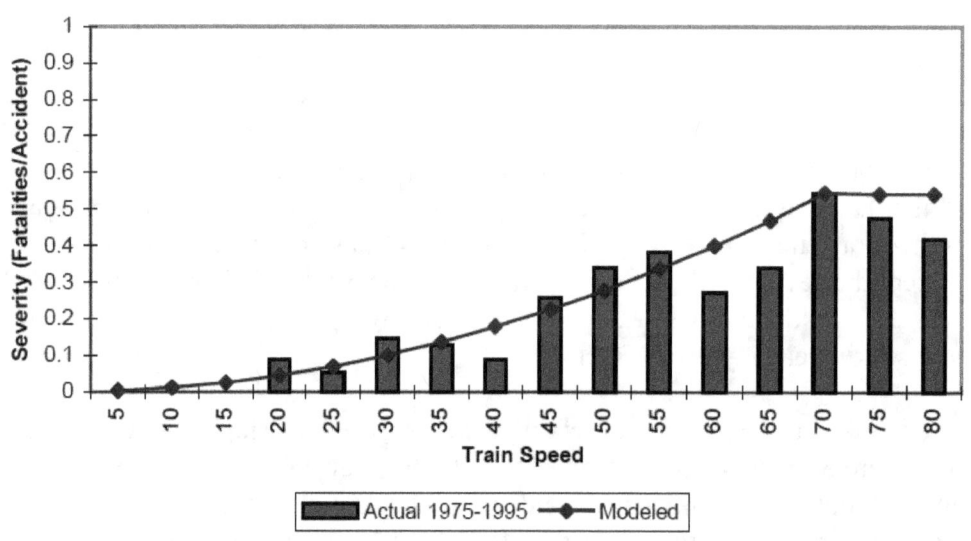

Figure 3-3. Fatalities per Accident on Trucks Struck by Passenger Train

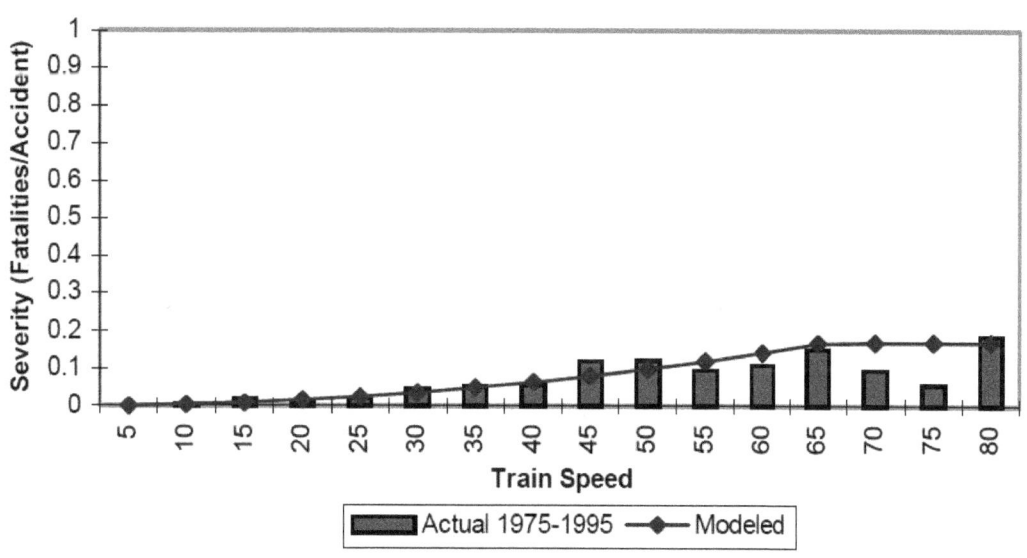

Figure 3-4. Fatalities per Accident on Truck-Trailers Struck by Passenger Train

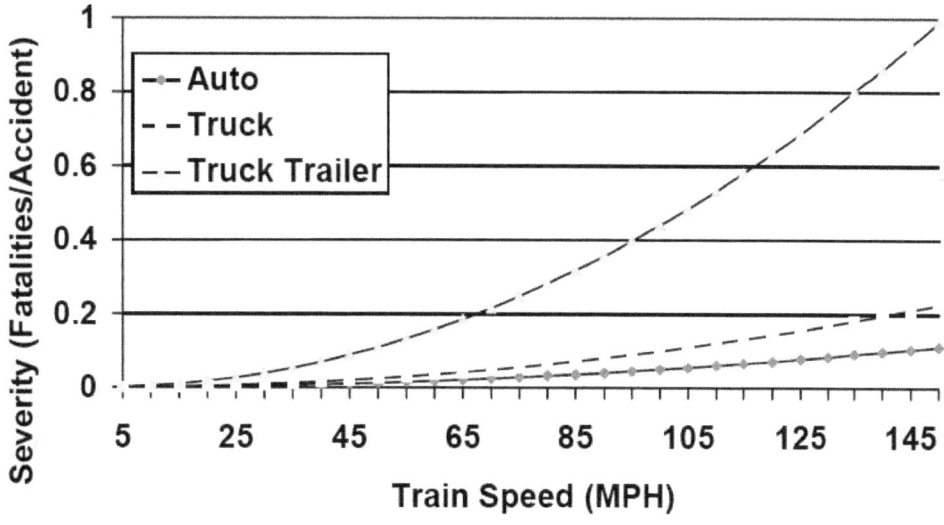

**Figure 3-5. Modeled Severity to Train Occupants (Impact Only, No Derailment);
Train Striking Highway Vehicle**

Additional harm to the train occupants can occur if the train derails. Therefore, the rail equipment accident data base was cross-indexed with the grade crossing data base to obtain data on derailments caused by grade crossing accidents. Since the format of the rail equipment data base changed after 1991, the 4 years 1992-1995 were used.

Of the 1,018 passenger train accidents at grade crossings in this period, there were 13 derailments. Of these, 10 were train striking truck trailer, 2 were train striking truck, and one was auto striking train. There were no fatalities on any of the trains. In examining the 19,267 crashes of all remaining types of trains at grade crossings, it was shown that there were 72 additional derailments. Again, there were no fatalities, and the majority involved truck trailers, followed by trucks and then autos. From the passenger train data, probabilities of a derailment of a passenger train striking a highway vehicle were derived as 14 percent for truck trailers, 2 percent for trucks, and 0.2 percent for autos. Since most of these derailments were of low severity, it was further assumed that only 5 percent were serious enough to be life-threatening.[1] Finally, assuming that the fatalities on a train resulting from a derailment are related to the square of the train speed, the relationship shown on Figure 3.6 indicates the additional number of fatalities incurred on the train if it is involved in a severe derailment. Additionally, the train speed may affect the probability of a severe derailment. In the absence of any fatality data, however, a flat rate, with the speed effects included in the severity curve, provides a reasonable estimate of the likely severity from derailment.

The probability that a train in a given crash will derail is actually a function of many factors. Perhaps the most important is the geometry of the crossing. In examining the risk on a corridor, crossings with sharp turns or steep embankments must be considered.

An additional note on interpreting the implications of this model. Consider a severity of 0.5 fatalities/accident as an example. While one fatality every two crashes could produce that severity level, it could also mean that there could be nine crashes without a fatality, and one where five people are killed.

---

[1] A sensitivity analysis was conducted regarding the percentage of severe derailments. If the proportion were increased to 20 percent, total risk would increase by 0.7 percent, and risk to train passenger by 6 percent. Even if it were assumed that all derailments were "severe," the total risk would increase by 4 percent, and risk to train passengers would increase by 36 percent, a relatively minor increase for 20 times more derailments.

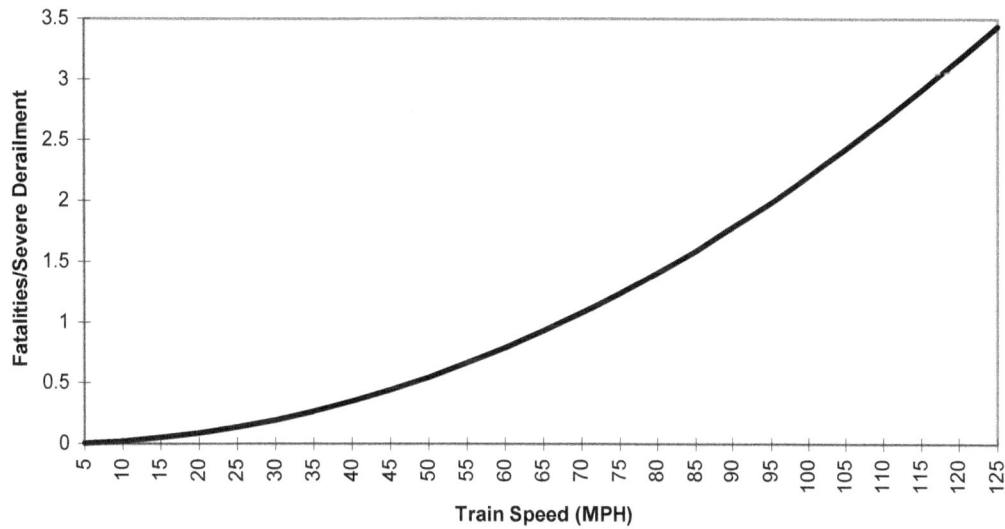

Figure 3-6. Additional Modeled Severity to Train Occupants in Severe Derailment

3.3.2 Highway Vehicle Into Train

This was a relatively infrequent crash mode, with generally extremely low harm to the occupants of the train, but often great severity to the highway vehicle.

First, consider the highway vehicle. While the severity is highly dependent on the speed of the vehicle, the train speed does not seem to contribute to severity. For example, historically, there have been a significant number of fatalities for highway vehicles striking a stopped train. Therefore, for this analysis, it was assumed that the severity to the vehicle occupants was independent of the train speed. It was further assumed that increasing the speed of the trains would not affect the severity on the highway vehicles. To determine the severity (expressed in predicted fatalities per accident), the accident data from 1975-1995, were examined to see how many of each accident type occurred, and the number of fatalities that resulted. For example, there were 751 cases of autos running into passenger trains, with 163 fatalities as a result, so that the severity was 163/751 = 0.217 fatalities/accident. Two sets of data were examined, vehicles into all trains, and vehicles into passenger trains, and the more severe result was used ("passenger train" data for autos and trucks, "all train" data for truck-trailers). These results are shown in Table 3-1.

Table 3-1. Severity of Vehicle-Into-Train Crashes

	Autos	Trucks	Truck Trailers
Vehicle Fatalities/Accident	0.217	0.16	0.091
Train Fatalities/Accident	0.01	0.01	0.01

15

In the 21 years of accident data from 1975 to 1995, there were no train fatalities resulting from any of the 984 cases of a train being struck by a highway vehicle [5]. Prior to 1975, there had been several tragic examples of fatalities resulting from this crash type, but changes in rail car crashworthiness make statistics from this era inapplicable to the current situation. Clearly, in the absences of any historical data, it is impossible to derive any empirical model. Since fatalities are still possible, however, particularly if the train derails, it was conservatively assumed that there was one train fatality per hundred accidents, for all vehicle types, including any harm from a possible derailment. This represents all the severity for train occupants in highway vehicle-into-train accidents on Figure 3-1.

3.4   SCENARIO WEIGHTS

In the preceding sections, the severity for each scenario on the fault tree was determined. To derive an overall severity figure, the distribution of these scenarios must be calculated, and the values combined. Again, the accident data base was used to derive these values.

Working down the tree, the first level is whether or not the train strikes the vehicle, or the vehicle strikes the train. For all types of trains, this distribution is around 75 percent and 25 percent, respectively. However, from the data for 1975-1995, looking only at passenger trains, 84 percent of the time the train struck the vehicle. Since this study focuses on passenger trains, and this leads to a more conservative result, these values were used.

Similarly, the distribution of highway vehicles involved in accidents with passenger trains was also used. Approximately 8 percent of these crashes involved pedestrians or motorcycles, but these are unlikely to cause deaths on the train, and also are unlikely to be more severe at speeds greater than 80 mph. Therefore, since this analysis focuses on the sensitivity of risk to train speed, accidents with pedestrians and motorcycles are not modeled here. Instead, it is assumed that all accidents fall into one of the three categories shown on the tree: autos, trucks, and truck trailers. The distributions are listed in Table 3-2. Vehicles such as school buses are not included here. Statistically, they comprise only a fraction of a percent of the accident problem, and so an analysis such as this would not give the problem much weight. However, it is essential that the risk to school bus passengers be adequately addressed, and so it should be considered on a qualitative rather than a quantitative basis.

Table 3-2. Distribution of Highway Vehicle Types

	Autos	Trucks	Truck Trailers
Percent of Vehicle Type	72.6	19.5	7.9

It is important to realize that the actual mix of vehicles at a particular crossing could have a major impact on the severity of accidents. A crossing used primarily by light vehicles

16

will have high severity for the highway vehicle passengers, and relatively low severity for the train. If, however, the crossing is used primarily by heavy trucks, the severity to the highway vehicle is lower, but the severity to the train increases. Figures 3-7 and 3-8 show the effect of vehicle mix on the severity to the highway vehicle and train respectively, while Figure 3-9 shows the effect on the total severity As one can see from the figure, even a shift from vehicle traffic consisting only of automobiles to one of all truck-trailers has a smaller effect on total severity than one might expect.

It should also be noted that crossings with significant traffic of special types of vehicles, e.g., school buses and hazardous material carriers, need to be assessed independently rather than on the "average severity" approach used here.

3.5 COMPOSITE SEVERITY

When the data from Sections 3.3 and 3.4 are combined, an overall severity curve can be determined. This is illustrated on Figure 3-10. The initial rapid slope is due to the fatalities in the highway vehicles. Above a train speed of 80 mph, the more gradual increase is due to the fatalities on the train.

By combining the severity in this section with the accident probability estimates in Section 2, the estimated risk at each crossing can be obtained. The following section examines some of the methods for reducing these risks.

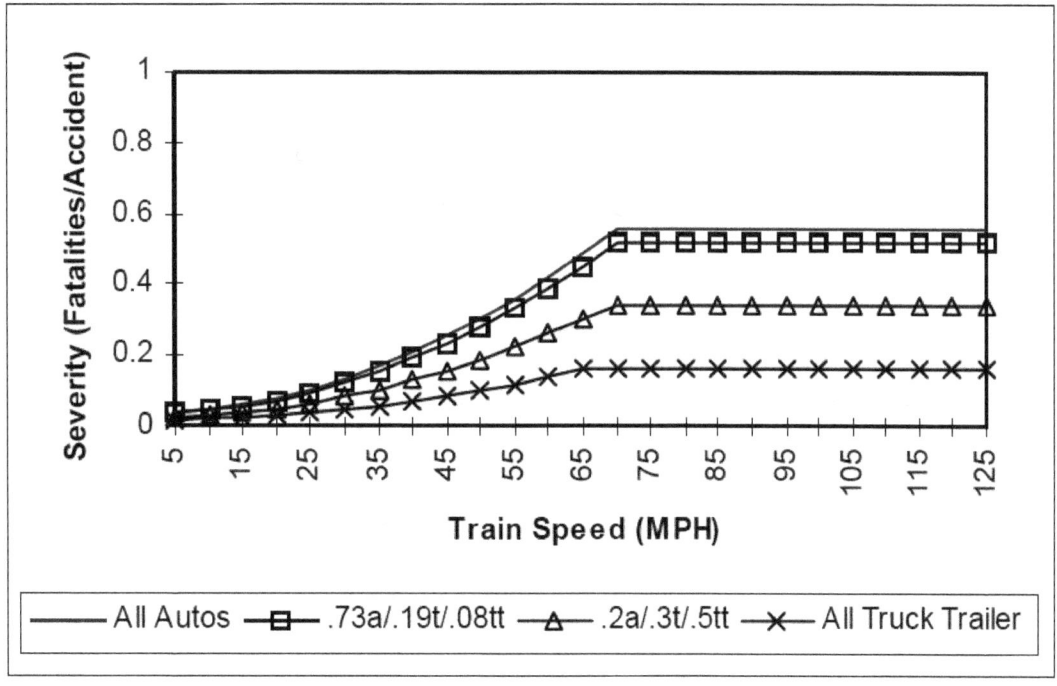

Figure 3-7. Total Predicted Severity to HV Occupants for Different Vehicle Mixes

17

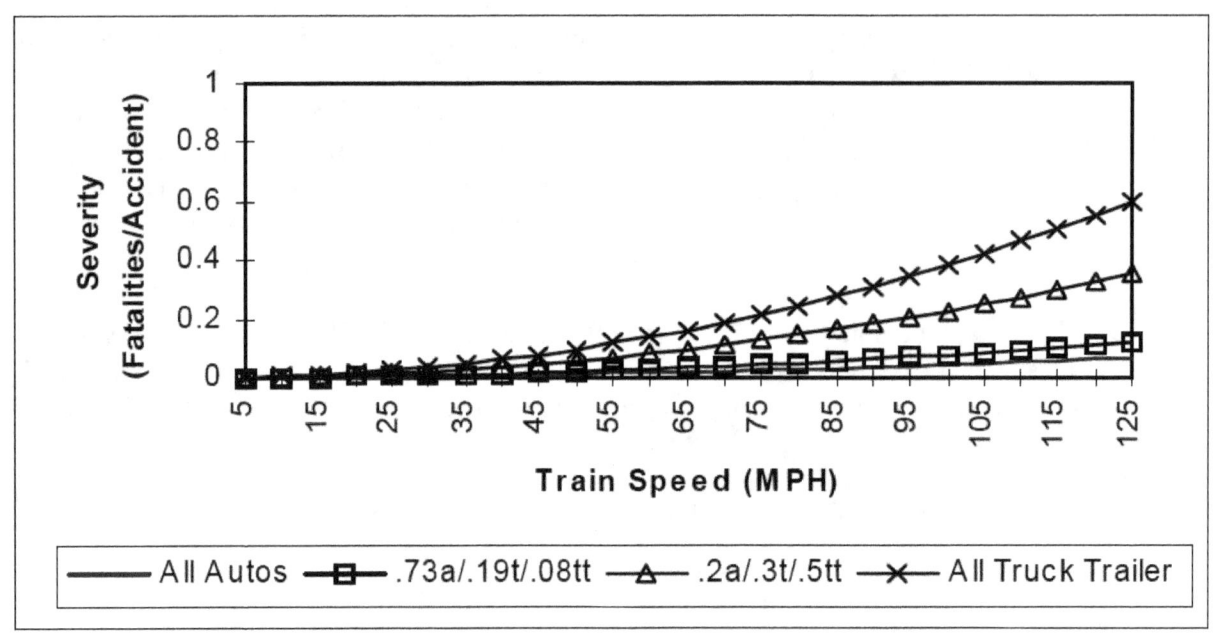

Figure 3-8. Total Predicted Severity to Train Occupants for Different Vehicle Mixes

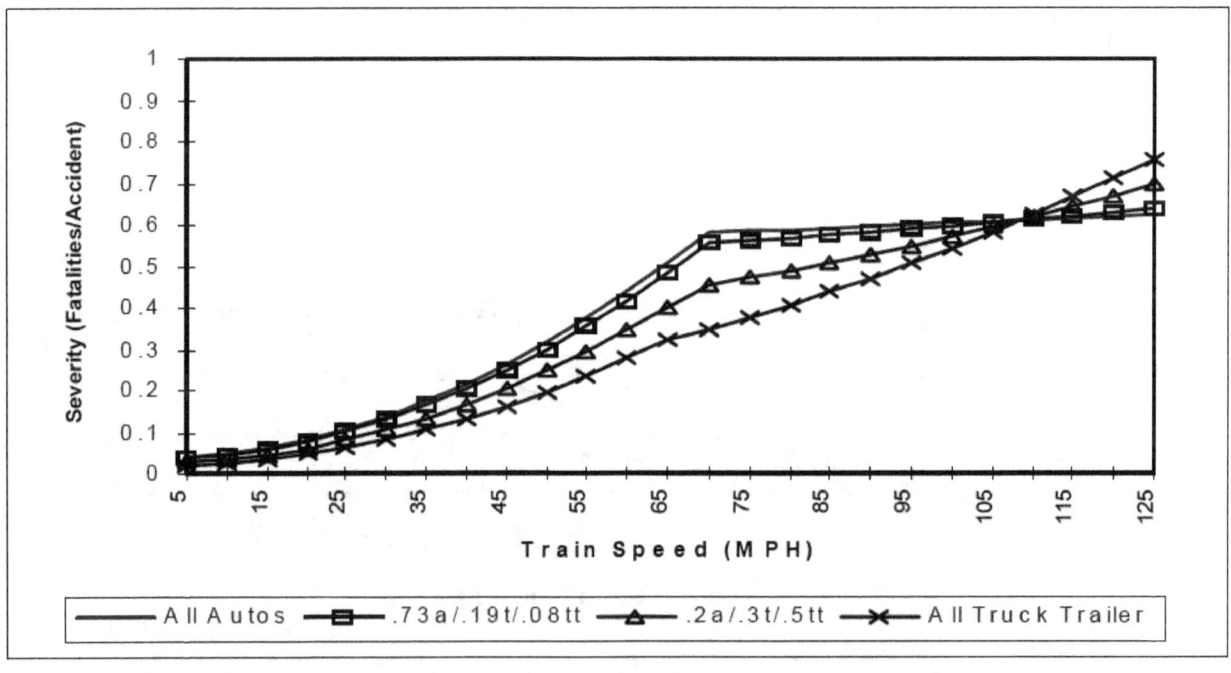

Figure 3-9. Predicted Aggregate Severity for Different Vehicle Mixes

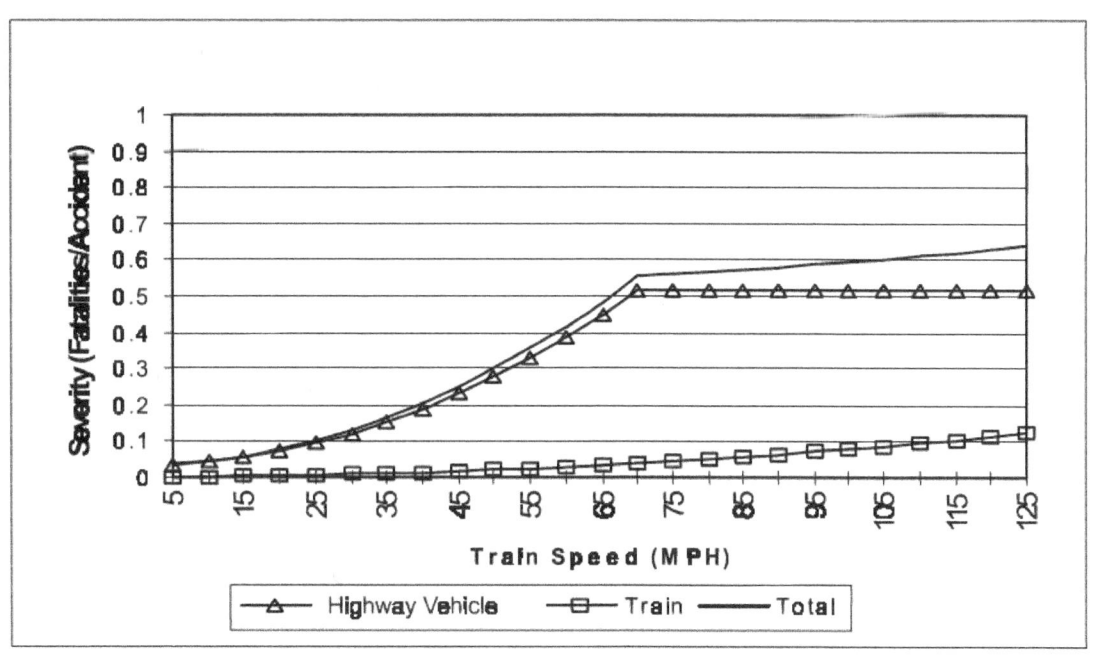

Figure 3-10. Total Predicted Aggregate Severity (Baseline Vehicle Mix)

4. EFFECTIVENESS OF GRADE CROSSING WARNING DEVICES

4.1 INTRODUCTION

The previous sections have described a method for quantifying risk at grade crossings. This section will present the approach used for determining how that risk can be decreased by improving the warning devices at grade crossings.

4.2 CHANGE IN ACCIDENT RATE USING THE PREDICTION MODEL

As described in Section 2, the accident prediction model was based on regression performed independently for each of the three warning types examined (passive, flashing lights, and gates). The "Rail-Highway Crossing Resource Allocation Procedure User's Guide" prescribes applying an effectiveness rate to the accident rate for the lesser warning to determine the accident rate with the new warning device. This approach was not used here for several reasons.

First, that method was not intended to deal with increases in speed. Since passive crossing accident rates in the model are dependent on speed, and active crossings are not, there is an ambiguity as to whether to apply the effectiveness before or after calculating the effects of the speed.

Second, since the accident history of the crossing was not used (for the reasons outlined in Section 2), it was assumed that in the steady state, two crossings with identical characteristics should have the same accident rate.

Finally, at least for the crossings to be examined in the following section, applying the accident prediction formula to the improved crossing rather than using the effectiveness numbers lead to a more conservative result. For example, putting gates on a particular passive crossing (in this case the Pirate Canoe crossing) results in a 75 percent effectiveness using the formula, rather than the 80-85 percent found in the user's manual. Similarly, changing a crossing with flashing lights (e.g., the Hamilton Paper crossing) to gates achieves an effectiveness of 41 percent, rather than the 69 percent in the manual.

4.3 EFFECTIVENESS AND COST OF OTHER WARNING DEVICES

While the regression model can be used as described above for gates and flashing lights, there is no formula that can be applied to advanced warning devices such as median barriers and four-quadrant gates. Therefore, effectiveness rates must be used instead.

The "Sealed Corridor" study conducted by the North Carolina Department of Transportation and the Norfolk Southern Corporation [7] examined the effectiveness of these devices. While the results are preliminary, they provide a reasonable approximation of the effectiveness of such systems. These values are shown in Table 4-1.

The cost estimates were based on values found in the literature [6,7,8]. It is assumed that all types of warning devices can be installed at all crossings, and that the cost is the same at each crossing, regardless of the particular geometry of that crossing.

Table 4-1. Effectiveness and Cost of Crossing Improvements

	Median Barriers	4-Quadrant Gates	Grade Separation
Effectiveness (Over Gates)	30%	40%	100%
Cost Estimate	$20,000	$125,000-250,000	$1,000,000-3,000,000

As for installing gates on passive crossings, the cost was also estimated at $125,000-250,000 as well, and as mentioned above, the effectiveness was determined using the accident prediction model.

Finally, for some low-volume passive crossings, the risk can be essentially eliminated by either closing the crossings or installing dispatcher controlled gates, or another form of locked gates. However, the "cost" of such modifications is heavily dependent on factors other than the equipment needed, such as whether or not alternate routes exist, the nature of the highway vehicle traffic at the crossing, etc. Therefore, no figures are given here.

The next section examines a section of the New York Empire Corridor, applying the methodology discussed.

5. APPLICATION OF METHODOLOGY TO EMPIRE CORRIDOR

5.1 INTRODUCTION

The Empire Corridor runs between New York City and Buffalo, New York. There is considerable interest in the effect of raising train speeds on a particular portion of this corridor along the Hudson River. New York State has a goal of eventually reducing the travel time between Albany and New York City to less than 2½ hours. The increased ridership and revenue could then be applied toward additional investments, leading to a zero-risk corridor with no at-grade crossings. However, before the train speed can be increased, improvements must be made to the Corridor so that even with the higher train speed, corridor safety is improved. Therefore, this 94-mile section of the Empire Corridor, located between Poughkeepsie and Albany, was chosen to illustrate the methodology described in this report.

5.2 SAFETY HISTORY

Since 1980, trains have been running at a maximum speed of 110 mph over sections of the Empire Corridor. While the train speed varies based on geometry and proximity to stations, most crossings have a maximum speed of 110, 95, or 90 mph. These are shown in Table 5-1.

In the 17 years of train operations at these higher speeds, there have been only three accidents at public crossings, with no fatalities. This includes 10 days in 1995, when trains were operated without incident at speeds as high as 125 mph during a special test.

The record at private crossings is much less encouraging. In the same period of time, there were 15 accidents at private crossings, resulting in 5 injuries and 5 fatalities. Two of these crossings subsequently have been closed; therefore, the accidents at these crossings are not included in the analysis. Figure 5-1 shows the distribution of the 16 accidents and 4 fatalities along the section studied.

Table 5-1. Current Speeds and Warning Devices

Crossing	Mile Post	Current Allowable Train Speed	Crossing Type
Manitou	46.04	80	Gated Public
King's Dock	47.40	80	Passive Private
Bank St.	62.55	80	Gated Public
Pirate Canoe	71.00	90	Passive Private
Captains 3	75.95	90	Gated Private
Private Rd.	81.00	95	Passive Private
Pok Yacht	81.59	90	Gated Private
River Rd.	83.70	95	Gated Public
Tivoli Dock	98.95	95	Gated Private
Clermont	100.70	95	Passive Private
Private Rd	102.60	90	Passive Private
Cheviot	103.70	90	Gated Public
Dock Rd.	106.10	90	Gated Public
Oak Hill	109.50	90	Passive Private
Hallenbeck	111.98	90	Passive Private
Broad St.	114.30	50	Gated Public
Ferry Rd.	121.95	90	Gated Public
Ice House	122.25	90	Passive Private
Stuyvesant	124.81	110	Gated Public
Hook Boat	126.98	110	Passive Private
Walsh's	133.85	110	Passive Private
Green Av.	134.00	110	Gated Public
Scott St.	134.20	110	Gated Public
Hamilton Printing	134.90	110	Flashing Lights Private
Staat's	137.20	110	Gated Public
Ablee's	139.10	110	Passive Private
Teller's	139.98	110	Gated Private

(Proposed High-Speed Section Shaded)

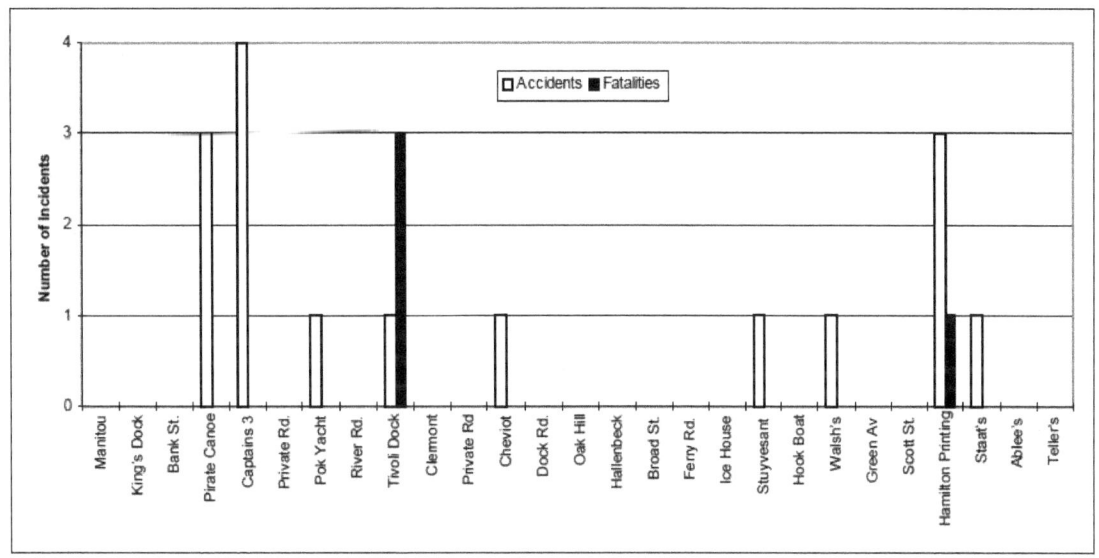

Figure 5-1. Safety History on Corridor Section Since 1980 (Crashes at Crossings Since Closed Excluded)

The five fatalities occurred as the result of the following three accidents:

- December 8, 1985. Tivoli Dock Crossing. Three Highway Vehicle Occupants Killed.
- January 27, 1990. Mile Post 133.05. One Highway Vehicle Occupant Killed. This crossing has since been closed.
- August 14, 1997. Hamilton Printing. One Highway Vehicle Occupant Killed.

No train occupant fatalities have occurred in this time frame.

5.3 ACCIDENT PREDICTION

Data were obtained from the Grade Crossing Inventory and the New York State Department of Transportation on the characteristics of 27 crossings in the area of interest, as shown on Figure 5-2. This section extends from Philipston (mile post 46), just north of Peekskill to Rensselaer (mile post 140), south of Albany. Table 5-1 lists the crossings, the mileposts, the current allowable train speed and the type of crossing. The data for each crossing were imparted into the accident prediction model described in Section 2. The Appendix lists this data, as well as the predicted accident rate at each crossing.

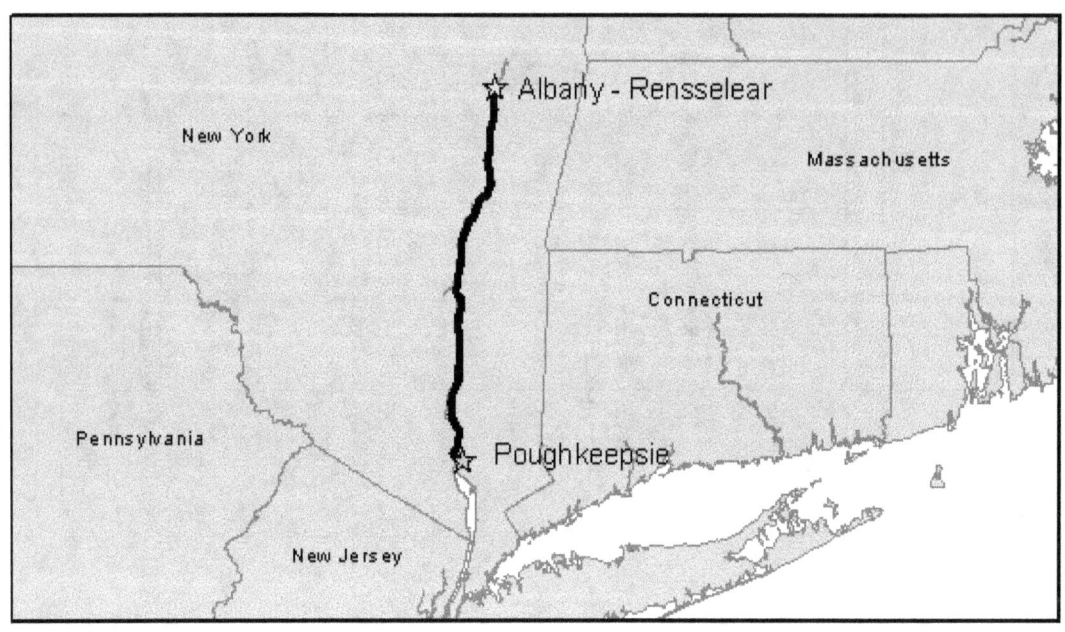

Figure 5-2. Map of Section of Empire Corridor Examined

5.4   DETERMINATION OF RISK

Section 3 presented the severity model derived for this project. Risk was derived by multiplying the accident rate by the severity for the given train speed at each crossing. Figure 5-3 shows the current estimated risk at each crossing as one travels north on the corridor. This risk is broken down into risk to train occupants, highway vehicle occupants, and the total of these two risk elements.

Figure 5-4 displays this same data as a running total of the cumulative risk as one traverses the corridor. By looking at the final bar, one can see that there are several thick bands, which represent higher risk crossings where improvements may have the greatest benefit.

Figures 5-5, 5-6, and 5-7 rank these data from lowest to highest risk, with Figure 5-5 based on total risk, and Figures 5-6 and 5-7 ranking on risk to train occupants and highway vehicle occupants respectively. Note that the same six crossings appear at the highest risk end of all three figures (Pirate Canoe, Hook Boat, Hamilton Printing, Bank Street, Manitou Road and Captains 3), although the order changes slightly.

26

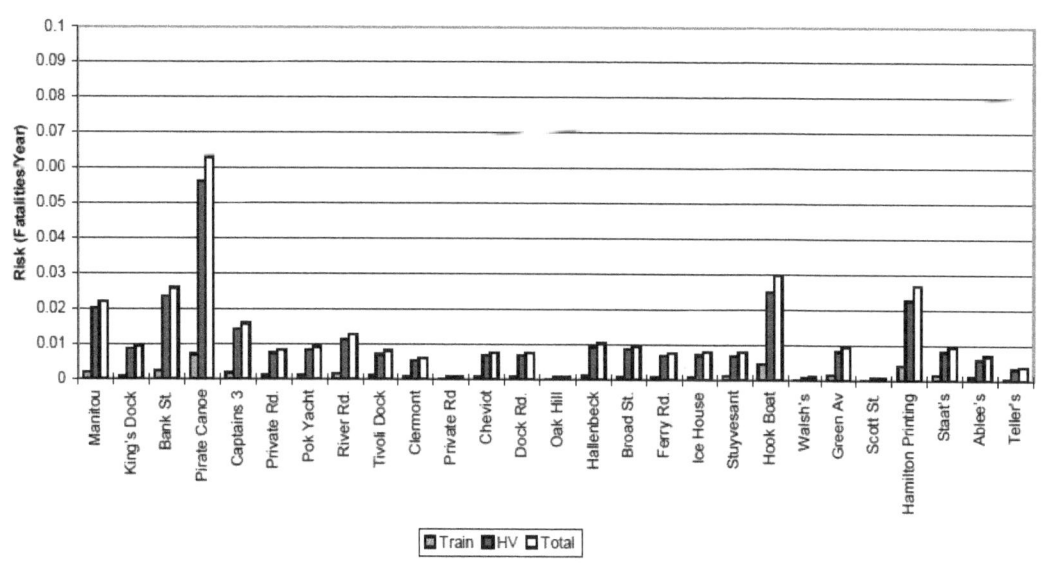

Figure 5-3. Estimated Risk at 27 Crossings (Shown South to North)

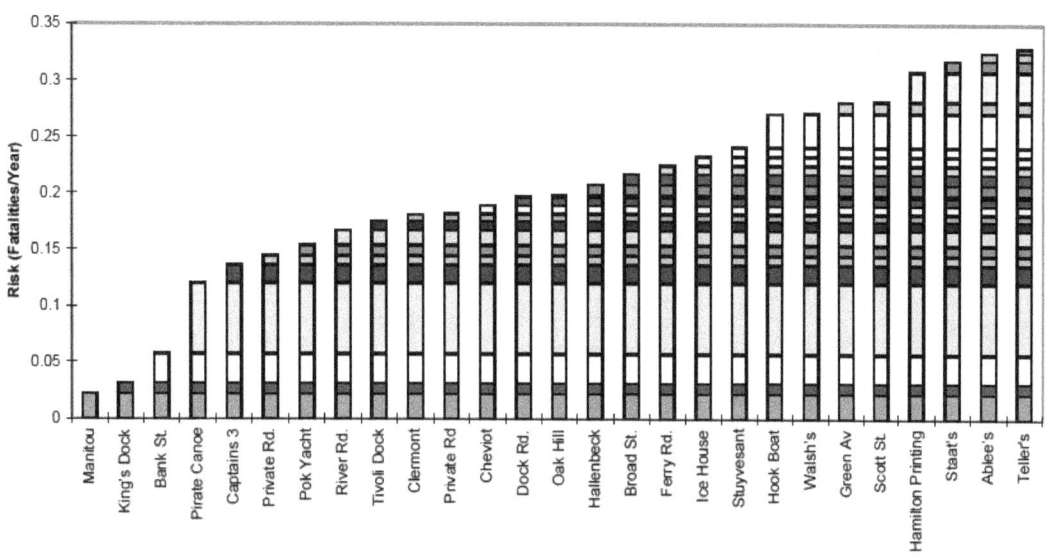

Figure 5-4. Cumulative Estimated Current Risk Travelling North

27

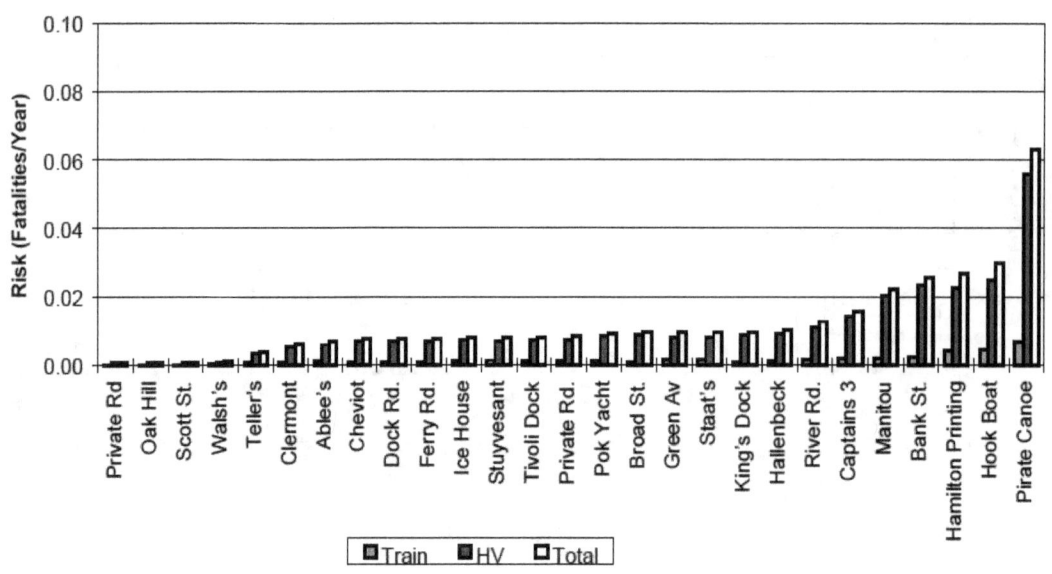

Figure 5-5. Estimated Risk at Each Crossing, Ranked by Total Risk

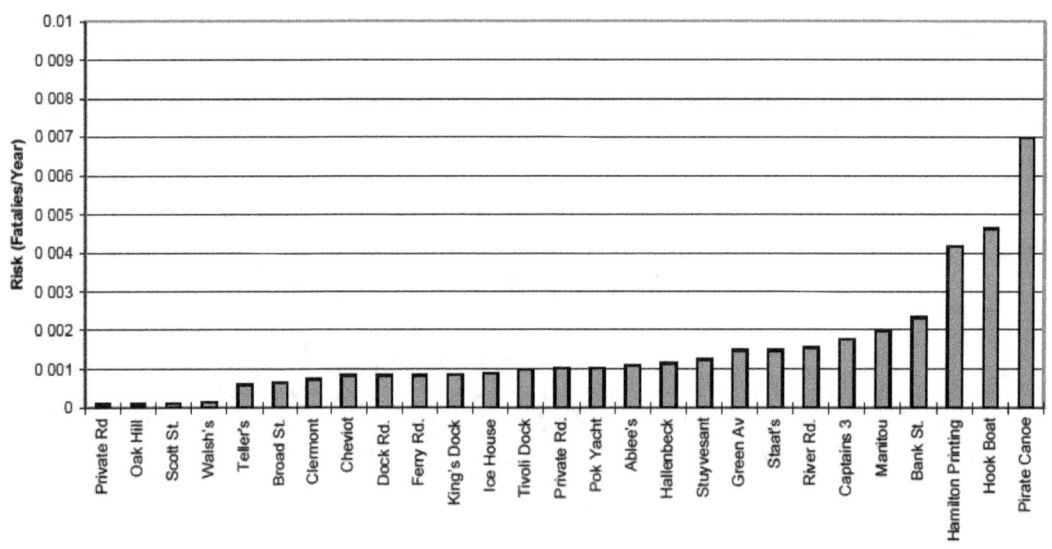

Figure 5-6. Estimated Risk to Train Occupants at Each Crossing, Ranked by Risk

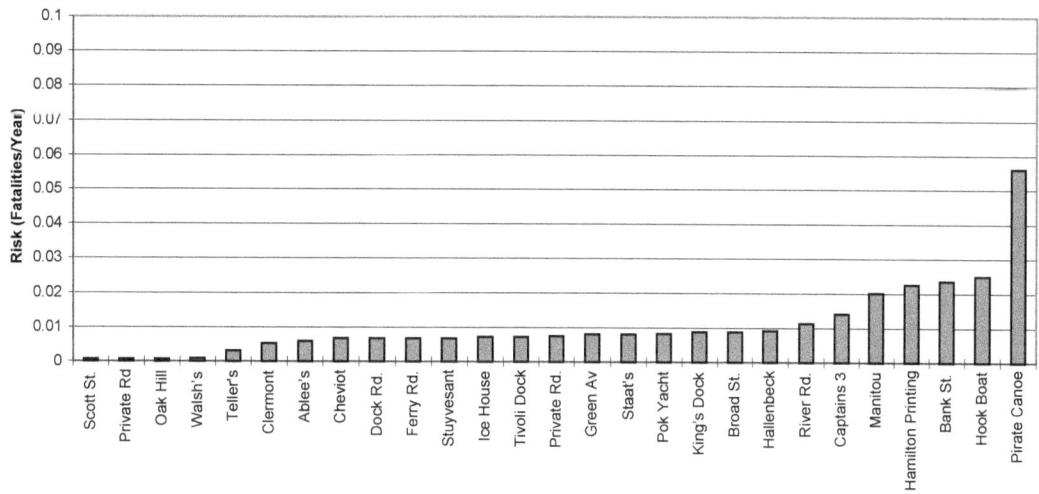

Figure 5-7. Estimated Risk to Highway Vehicle Occupants at Each Crossing

5.5   MODEL VALIDATION

Risk for the model is defined in terms of fatalities and is derived from the number of accidents and the severity (number of fatalities) of those accidents. Over the 18-year period reviewed, there were 16 accidents at the crossings still open, a rate of 0.89 per year. (Crossings that were closed were not included in calculating either the actual or predicted amounts.) The model would predict, after adjusting the coefficients of the prediction formulas, 10.9 accidents over the same 18 years. Some improvements may have been made at crossings during the review period, which would account for the variation.

In the 18-year period, there were four fatalities at these crossings, or 0.22 fatalities per year and 0.25 fatalities/accident. The model predicts 5.9 fatalities over the same period. These predicted fatalities – the risk – are determined by calculating the expected fatalities per year at each crossing, summing over all crossings to obtain a 0.33 rate, and then multiplying by 18 years to obtain 5.9 fatalities per year (0.33 x 18).

It is tempting to appraise model validity by comparing actual to predicted values, as given above, for accidents and fatalities. For reasons to be discussed, however, such comparisons should not serve as a test of model validity, or even indicate that it is necessary to establish "validity" in such a manner. (Also, it might be pointed out that because accident and particularly fatality counts are small for both actual and predicted values, absolute differences are small, but large in percentage terms. This makes validity assessment under any conditions problematic.)

The risk assessment model is intended as an analytic methodology to provide guidance in allocating the scare funds available to upgrade warning levels in a manner as to reduce

29

the most risk per unit of funds. The relative scaling of risk among a group of candidate crossings may be all that is needed; and not an absolute value which tracks the historical account, provided that the model does not exhibit a bias of over- or under-predicting one or several crossings among the 27.

What the risk model lacks is an adjustment based on the actual experience. A number of improvements have been made to crossings over the period, including the introduction of some active warning device systems. The crossings are also equipped with special signs warning "high-speed trains," and, in some cases, limited storage space for cars between the tracks and Route 9J. An historical adjustment makes allowances for difficult-to-quantify crossing characteristics like road and track geometry, sight distance, distractions, signage, and sidings. And over an 18-year period, the model could not account for differences in driver or train operating characteristics. These changes essentially shift the parameter values of the model. Without the historical adjustment, the model prediction should not be expected to equal the actual experience, particularly for a small group of crossings such as the 27 of this application. Yet, the model still can provide guidance in allocating funds among the crossings by upgrading warnings based on relative risk.

5.6   PROPOSED HIGH-SPEED SECTION

It has been proposed that the maximum train speed should be increased from 110 mph to 125 mph along a 15-mile section of this corridor, from Stuyvesant to Teller. Figure 5-8 shows the location of the nine crossings included within this section of the corridor.

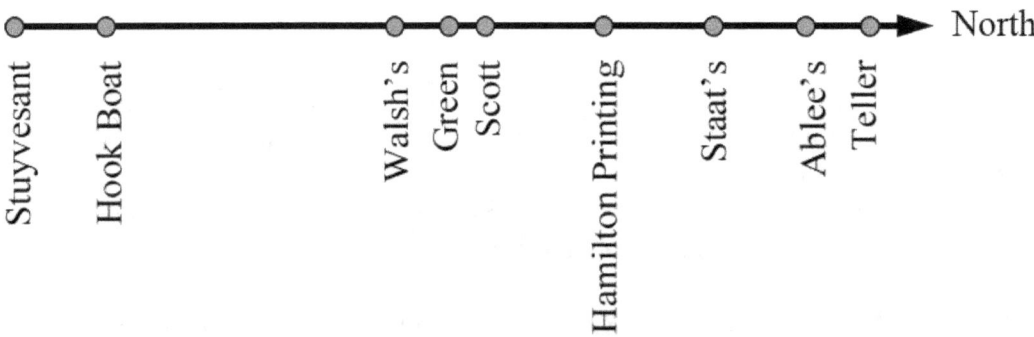

Figure 5-8. Detail of Proposed High-Speed Section

In addition, one crossing outside of the high-speed section currently at 50 mph (Broad Street) will be increased to 60 mph.

Figure 5-9 shows the risk at these crossings if the speed were increased without changing the current warning systems or crossing configurations. As could be expected, the risk increases at each crossing, although the increase is relatively modest.

30

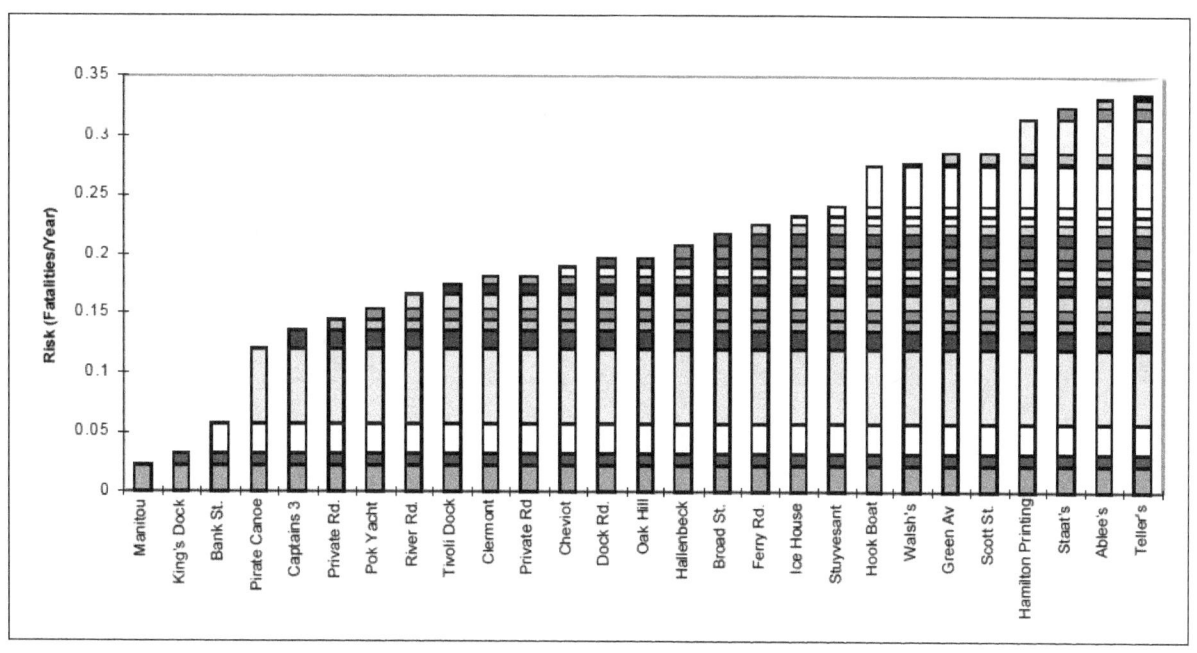

Figure 5-9. Risk at Each Crossing with Proposed Speed Increases

According to the current guidelines for high-speed train operations, these nine 125-mph crossings would have to meet the stringent requirements set out in Table 1-1. There are no currently available systems that satisfy these requirements, so the crossings would need to be either grade-separated or closed. If the risk at these nine crossings is reduced to zero, the total predicted risk on the 27 crossing section would become 0.23 fatalities per year. The cost of such changes would be high. However, since the vehicle traffic at the Hamilton Printing crossing is 250 vehicles per day, and Green Avenue and Staat's Island each average about 50 vehicles per day, closing is not an acceptable option and grade separation would be needed, at a total cost of $3 to $9 million. As discussed in Section 4.3, estimating the cost for the remaining six crossings is difficult, but the total cost could increase substantially.

5.7   SIX HIGHEST-RISK CROSSINGS

The analysis in Section 5.4 highlighted the six crossings that displayed the highest risk regardless of whether or not total risk or risk to either the train or highway vehicle is considered. This section further examines these crossings.

Figure 5-10 compares the risk at these six crossings to that at all of the remaining crossings. These six alone account for significantly more than half the total risk on the entire 96-mile section studied. Figures 5-11 and 5-12 show that this is also true when considering risk only on the train or the highway vehicle.

31

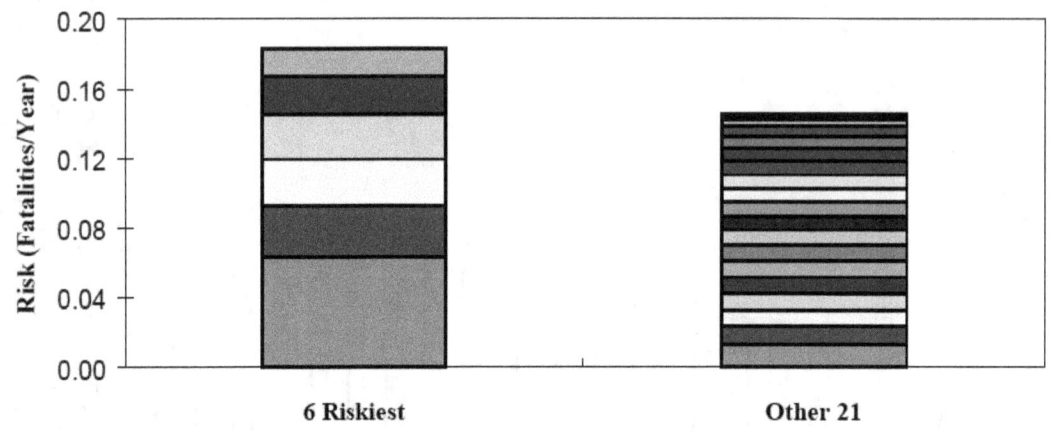

Figure 5-10. Comparison of Total Risk: 6 Highest-Risk Crossings vs. Remaining 21

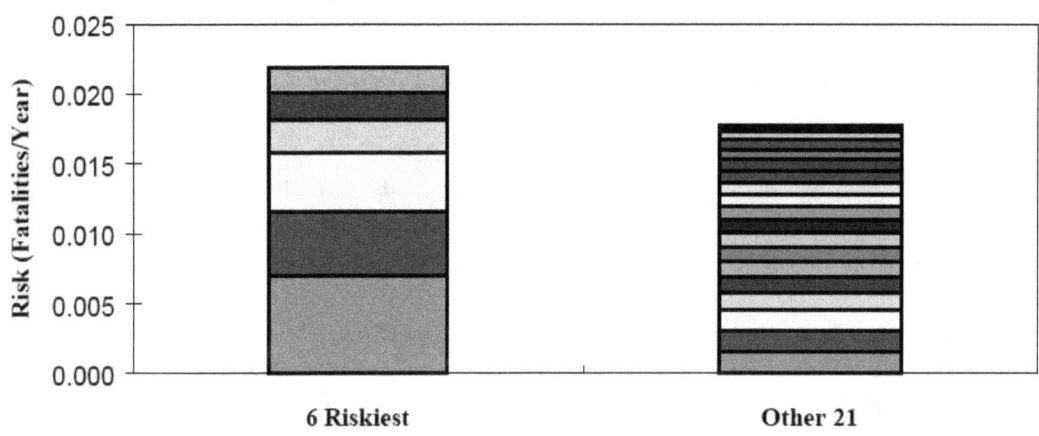

Figure 5-11. Comparison of Risk on Train Only: 6 Highest-Risk Crossings vs. Remaining 21

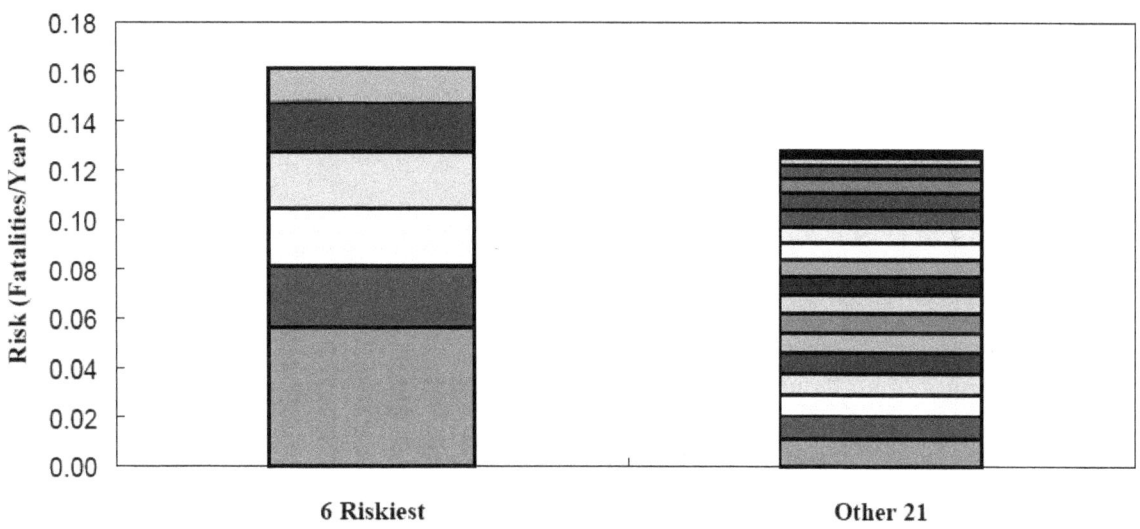

Figure 5-12. Comparison of Risk on Highway Vehicle Only: 6 Highest-Risk Crossings vs. Remaining 21

Table 5-2 shows some of the details of these six crossings. Only two of these six are in the high-speed section, and half of the crossings have gates. Also, four of these six are private crossings.

Table 5.2 Details of the 6 Highest-Risk Crossings

Crossing	Private/Public	Current Warning	Current Speed	Proposed Speed
Pirate	Private	Passive	90 mph	90 mph
Hamilton	Private	Flashing Lights	110 mph	125 mph
Hook	Private	Passive	110 mph	125 mph
Bank	Public	2-Quad Gates	80 mph	80 mph
Manitou	Public	2-Quad Gates	80 mph	80 mph
Captains 3	Private	2-Quad Gates	90 mph	90 mph

Based on the data in Section 4, if the train speed were increased as proposed, and each of these crossings were improved so that the crossings that are currently passive or have only flashing lights had two-quadrant gates instead, and the currently gated crossing became four-quadrant gates, the total risk on the entire section examined would be reduced to 0.23 fatalities per year. The cost of these upgrades is generally in the $125,000 to $250,000 range, for a total of $750, 000 to $1.5 million.

Figure 5-13 shows the cumulative total risk with the increased speed and the improvements described above. Comparing this with Figure 5-4, the baseline case, the bands on the bars are much more uniform, with no prominent wide bands of high risk as before.

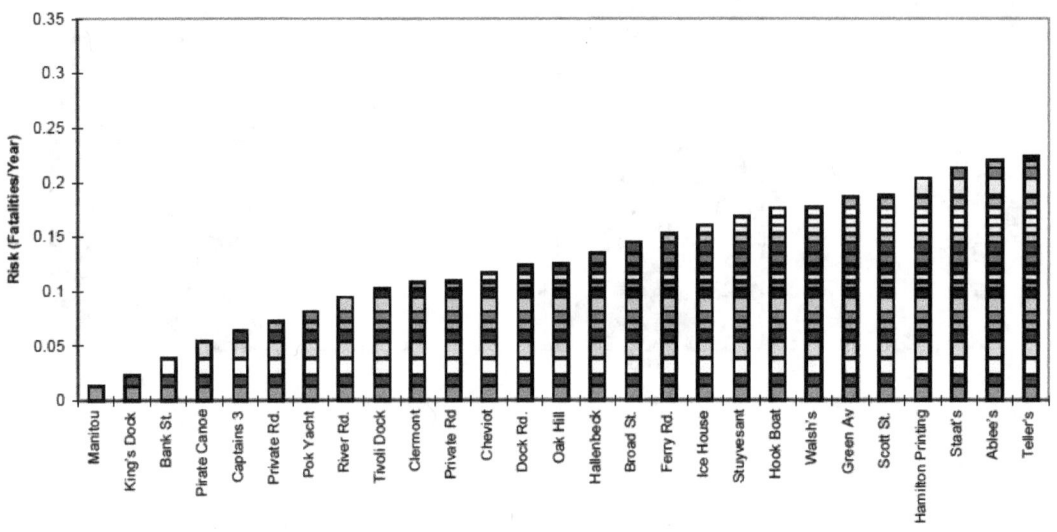

Figure 5-13. Cumulative Total Risk with Increased Train Speed and Six Improved Crossings

5.8   COMPARISON OF RISK REDUCTION STRATEGIES

Figure 5-14 compares the baseline risk, the high-speed proposal, the risk following application of the current guidelines, and the risk if the six riskiest crossings are improved. As can be seen, similar levels of risk result from both improvement schemes. The costs are quite different, however. The high-end estimate to address the six high-risk crossings is still only half the lowest estimate for following the guidelines for the 125-mph crossings. Table 5-3 summarizes these results.

Table 5-3. Summary of Results

Strategy	Improvements	Cost	Risk at 125 mph
Eliminate All High-Speed Crossings	3 Grade Separations 6 Closures	$3-9 Million +	0.23 fatalities/year
Improve Six Highest Risk Crossings	3 Upgrades to 2-Quad 3 Upgrades to 4-Quad	$0.75-1.5 Million	0.23 fatalities/year

34

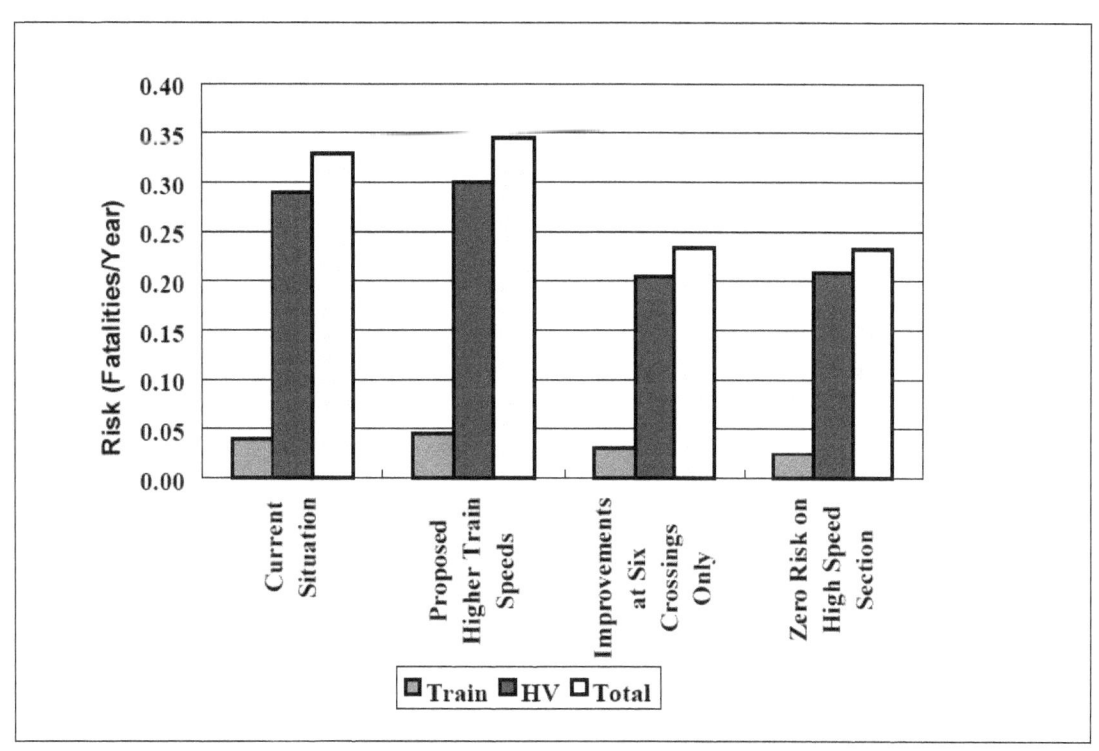

Figure 5-14. Comparison of Total Risk for Risk-Reduction Strategies

6.   CONCLUSIONS AND RECOMMENDATIONS

6.1   GENERAL COMMENTS

The risk to train passengers from grade crossing accidents does not increase as dramatically with train speed as one might initially expect. Passenger trains are significantly crashworthy and newer trains promise even greater levels of protection. There have been eight fatalities on passenger trains in grade crossing accidents from 1979 to 1995. Furthermore, no fatalities resulted from a highway vehicle striking a train in 20 years of data. Available data suggest that 110 mph is not exceptionally more risky than 80 mph. Finally, there does not seem to be reason to believe that discontinuous changes in risk occur above 110 mph; rather, severity most likely increases smoothly. Risk is dominated by exposure – the number of highway vehicles and trains using a given crossing. Conventional warning systems significantly reduce the probability of accidents. In preliminary tests, new warning systems such as four-quadrant gates and median barriers reduce even further the rate at which motor vehicle drivers violate crossing devices.

6.2   SUGGESTED ACTIONS FOR THE EMPIRE CORRIDOR

Examining the results in Section 5 leads to two conclusions. First, the increase in risk due to the proposed increases in train speed can be more than offset by implementing fairly standard crossing improvements. Second, the total risk on the section of the Corridor examined is driven by several high-risk crossings, some of them located outside of the high-speed section. By improving the highest-risk crossings, regardless of the maximum train speed, the greatest benefit can be realized.

6.3   SUGGESTED MODIFICATIONS TO THE FRA GUIDELINES

The FRA guidelines should offer additional flexibility to employ alternative risk reduction options, especially in the 110-125 mph speed regime. As indicated by this study, train speed can be increased, while significantly reducing risk, by proper application of warning devices and at a cost less than required by application of the FRA guidelines. Permission to use alternative options should be based on site-specific, objective analyses of the risks, using an approach such as that presented in this study.

Implementing the guidelines would achieve high levels of grade crossing safety. These levels, however, are not immediately attainable. What is needed is an incremental migration from the existing practices to ones leading to improved safety. By examining the particulars of the specific crossings, including train speed, as well as other factors, one can effect the greatest increase in safety, until there are sufficient resources to fully implement the guidelines.

6.4 EFFECTIVENESS OF NEW GRADE CROSSING TREATMENTS

While the best available data were used to estimate the effectiveness of new types of grade crossing treatment, such as four-quadrant gates and median barriers, these data are still preliminary. More research is needed into these and other approaches that offer potential for risk reduction at lower cost than grade separation. With data on the costs and effectiveness of these systems, the methodology presented in this report can be used to allocate available crossing improvement funds to effect the greatest possible improvement in safety for a given corridor.

APPENDIX. BASELINE STATISTICS ON EXAMINED CROSSINGS AND PREDICTED ACCIDENT RATE

Name	AADT	Train Mvmt	Main Tracks	Day Trains	Hwy Paved	Max Spd	Hwy Type	Hwy Lanes	Predicted Accidents
Gated Public:									
Manitou	167	68	2	41	1	80	6	2	0.03891
Bank St.	281	68	2	41	1	80	6	2	0.045346
River Rd.	143	22	2	13	1	95	6	2	0.021778
Cheviot	25	22	2	13	1	90	6	2	0.013039
Dock Rd.	25	22	2	13	1	90	6	2	0.013039
Broad St.	500	22	2	13	1	50	6	2	0.031474
Ferry Rd.	25	22	2	13	1	90	6	2	0.013039
Stuyvesant	25	22	2	13	1	110	6	2	0.013039
Green Av	50	20	2	13	1	110	6	2	0.015545
Scott St.	0	20	2	13	1	110	6	2	0.001269
Staat's	50	20	2	13	1	110	6	2	0.015545
Flashing Lights, Private:									
Hamilton Printing	250	22	2	13	1	110	6	2	0.043714
Passive Crossings:									
King's Dock	2	68	2	41	2	80	6	2	0.016814
Pirate Canoe	50	68	2	41	1	90	6	2	0.108447
Private Rd.	5	22	2	13	2	95	6	2	0.01425
Clermont	2	22	2	13	2	95	6	2	0.010162
Private Rd	0	22	2	13	2	90	6	2	0.001327
Oak Hill	0	22	2	13	2	90	6	2	0.001327
Hallenbeck	10	22	2	13	2	90	6	2	0.017714
Ice House	5	22	2	13	2	90	6	2	0.013711
Hook Boat	20	22	2	13	1	110	6	2	0.048485
Walsh's	0	22	2	13	2	110	6	2	0.001548
Ablee's	2	22	2	13	2	110	6	2	0.011407
Gated Private Crossings:									
Captains 3	50	68	2	41	1	90	6	2	0.027288
Pok Yacht	50	22	2	13	1	90	6	2	0.015987
Tivoli Dock	30	22	2	13	1	95	6	2	0.013757
Teller's	2	22	2	13	2	110	6	2	0.006209

REFERENCES

1. Luedeke, J.F. "Evaluation of Highway-Railroad Grade Crossing Decision Methodologies, Volume 4: Safety of Highway-Railroad Grade Crossings on High-Speed Guided Ground Transportation Corridors," Battelle. Unpublished Draft Report to Volpe National Transportation Systems Center, August 7, 1997.

2. Code of Federal Regulations, 49CFR, Subpart 213.347(b), Part II, Track Safety Standards; Final Rule. Federal Railroad Administration, Department of Transportation, Office of the Federal Register, National Archives and Records Administration, Vol. 63, No. 119, June 22, 1998.

3. Farr, E. "Rail-Highway Crossing Resource Allocation Procedure, User's Guide, Third Edition," Implementation Package. DOT/FRA/OS-87/10, August 1987.

4. Tyrell, D. Volpe National Transportation Systems Center. Personal Communication. Discussion of results of data analysis performed to support train car side impact study, June 1997.

5. Tyrell, D., and J.C. Dorsey. "Consequences of Highway-Railroad at-Grade Crossing Collisions." Project Memorandum, Volpe National Transportation Systems Center, October 1995.

6. Mead, K. "Railroad Safety: Status of Efforts to Improve Railroad Crossing Safety," GAO Report/RCED-95-191, August 1995.

7. Reilly, M.J., R.H. Hines, and A.E.Tanner. "Rail Safety/Equipment Crashworthiness, Volume 1: A Systems Analysis of Injury Minimization in Rail Systems," Report No. FRA/ORD-77/73, I, July 1978.

8. Worley, P., and A. Mastrangelo. "Sealed Corridor," Draft Study Results, North Carolina Department of Transportation and Norfolk Southern Corporation Report, 1997.

www.ingramcontent.com/pod-product-compliance
Lightning Source LLC
Chambersburg PA
CBHW052015280526
45793CB00005B/990